A Conclusive Study on the Issue of Hijrah & Separating from the Polytheists

Compiled by:
Husayn bin 'Awdah Al-'Awaayishah

With Appendixes Containing the Statements of the Contemporary Scholars on Hijrah

First Edition: March 2006 / Safar 1427H

Copyright by Al-Ibaanah Book Publishing, USA

All rights reserved. No part of this publication may be reproduced in any language, stored in any retrieval system or transmitted in any form or by any means, whether electronic, mechanic, photocopying, recording or otherwise, without the express permission of the copyright owner.

Cover Design: 'Abdus-Salaam Walker
aslconcept@earthlink.net

Printed By: Sanatech Printers, NY

Published by: Al-Ibaanah Book Publishing

Translated by: Abu Maryam Isma'eel Alarcon

Web Site: www.al-ibaanah.com

E-Mail: info@al-ibaanah.com

Subject: Worship

Please visit us on the web at: **www.al-ibaanah.com** for free access to hundreds of Islamic articles and scholarly biographies, as well as dozens of downloadable e-books.

Note: The source used for the translation of this book was the first edition published by Dar Usayd ('Amman, Jordan) in 1993. A newer edition (1423H) published by Dar Ibn Hazm was also used for reference. The Noble Qur'aan (Dar-us-Salam) was used for the English rendering of the meaning of Qur'anic verses (with additions/alterations).

Table of Contents

Publisher's Foreword

All praise is for Allaah and may His praises and peace be on the last of His Messengers (i.e. Muhammad), his family and all of his Companions. To proceed:

This is a translation of the book *"Al-Fasl-ul-Mubeen fee Mas'alat-il-Hijrah wa Mufaaraqat-il-Mushrikeen"* **[A Conclusive Study on the Issue of Hijrah and Separating from the Polytheists]** written by the well-known student of knowledge, Husayn bin 'Awdah Al-'Awaayishah. Many of the readers may already be aware of the author due to the large amount of his works that have been translated into the English language. However, this book differs from all of them due to the fact that it consists more of a research on the issue at hand and a relaying of the statements of the scholars from the past on this subject.

This is explained well by the author in his introduction, when he says: "So due to Hijrah having the high position and status that it has, I decided to write what I could on it, seeking to voice myself through the words of our past scholars and Fuqahaa, by way of their books on Tafseer, Hadeeth and Fiqh. This was so that the conclusive opinion derived can be based on the upholders of knowledge and so that the resulting view can be from its people."

And he has spoken truthfully as the majority of his work consists of statements of the well-known scholars of the past on Hijrah, while some chapters have been added from the author's own words to incite the readers and summarize what the scholars have stated.

As an added benefit, thirteen appendixes have been placed at the end of the book containing the words of the present day scholars on Hijrah - those who have passed away and those still alive - so as to make this book as comprehensive on the subject as possible.

Indeed, this is the first time, according to our observation, that such a book of this magnitude - in that it compiles the statements of the Muslim scholars, past and present - has ever been presented on this subject in the English language.

The main reason such a project was undertaken was due to the urgent need for a clarification on this tremendous act of worship since, as the Prophet ﷺ has foretold us, Islaam has and continues to enter every household and area and people are accepting Islaam while in the Lands of the Disbelievers. So the questions constantly arise and the discussions grow long on the aspect of Hijrah - is it obligatory or recommended or neither of the two? And the issue has become such that the people have become divided into two sides - one that absolutely mandates it on the people, paying no attention to its guidelines, etiquettes or detailed matters, and another that completely disregards it and considers it as being something abrogated and no longer part of the Religion.

However, the true way of Ahlus-Sunnah wal-Jamaa'ah is that of the middle course, between the two extremities. And this is what is outlined in detail here, such that the scholars, past and present, have spoken elaborately on this subject, clarifying it from every angle. So you will find in their statements a clarification on the rules of Hijrah, the types of Hijrah, the categories of people with regards to it, the definitions of the "Land of Islaam" and the "Land of Shirk", those exempted from Hijrah, the conditions for residing in the Lands of Disbelief, and much more.

Adding to the benefit, as stated above, is the words of the scholars of recent and present times, which give the reader remarkable insight into the issues of Hijrah as they apply in modern times, for indeed, even though the basis and rules of Hijrah do not change, its manner and surrounding factors change throughout the course of time. And this is evident in their statements, so refer to them. One may ask why there is a need for so many statements from so many different scholars on the same topic. But one only needs to read their statements to realize the variety and diversity of points of benefit raised by them, all of which serve to support one another and assist the reader in getting a universal understanding of Hijrah and all of its facets.

We ask Allaah to make this unique effort sincerely for His sake and to make it a means for clarifying the truth regarding this magnificent act of worship to the masses of English-speaking Muslims. Verily, He is the All-Hearer of supplications and the Responder to them.

Al-Ibaanah Book Publishing

Introduction to the Book

Verily, all praise is due to Allaah. We praise Him, we seek His assistance and we ask Him for His forgiveness. And we seek refuge in Allaah from the evils of our souls and the evils of our actions. Whoever Allaah guides, there is no one that can lead him astray, and whoever is led astray, there is no one that can guide him. I bear witness that there is no deity that has the right to be worshipped except Allaah - He stands alone and without any partners. And I bear witness that Muhammad ﷺ is His slave and Messenger.

يَا أَيُّهَا الَّذِينَ آمَنُوا اتَّقُوا اللَّهَ حَقَّ تُقَاتِهِ وَلاَ تَمُوتُنَّ إِلاَّ وَأَنتُم مُّسْلِمُونَ

"O you who believe, fear Allaah as He ought to be feared and do not die except as Muslims." [Surah Aali 'Imraan: 103]

يَا أَيُّهَا النَّاسُ اتَّقُوا رَبَّكُمُ الَّذِي خَلَقَكُم مِّن نَّفْسٍ وَاحِدَةٍ وَخَلَقَ مِنْهَا زَوْجَهَا وَبَثَّ مِنْهُمَا رِجَالاً كَثِيراً وَنِسَاء وَاتَّقُوا اللَّهَ الَّذِي تَسَاءلُونَ بِهِ وَالأَرْحَامَ إِنَّ اللَّهَ كَانَ عَلَيْكُمْ رَقِيبًا

"O you who believe, fear your Lord who created you from a single soul (Aadam), and from it, He created his wife, and from them, He created many men and women. Fear Allaah through whom you demand your mutual rights, and (do not cut off the relations of) the wombs. Surely, Allaah is ever an All-Watcher over you." [Surah An-Nisaa: 1]

يَا أَيُّهَا الَّذِينَ آمَنُوا اتَّقُوا اللَّهَ وَقُولُوا قَوْلًا سَدِيدًا . يُصْلِحْ لَكُمْ أَعْمَالَكُمْ وَيَغْفِرْ لَكُمْ ذُنُوبَكُمْ وَمَن يُطِعْ اللَّهَ وَرَسُولَهُ فَقَدْ فَازَ فَوْزًا عَظِيمًا

"O you who believe, fear Allaah and be truthful and precise in your speech. He will rectify your deeds for you and forgive you of your sins. And whoever obeys Allaah and His Messenger has achieved a great success." [Surah Al-Ahzaab: 70-71]

As for what follows, then indeed, the best speech is the Book of Allaah, and the best guidance is the guidance of Muhammad ﷺ. And the most evil of affairs are newly invented matters, for indeed every newly invented matter is an innovation, and every innovation is a misguidance. And every misguidance is in the Hellfire. To proceed:

Allaah has indeed commanded us to obey and worship Him, saying:

وَمَا خَلَقْتُ الْجِنَّ وَالْإِنسَ إِلَّا لِيَعْبُدُونِ

"And I have not created the jinn and mankind except that they should worship Me." [Surah Adh-Dhaariyaat: 56]

And indeed from among the most honorable forms of worship that our Prophet ﷺ and his Companions performed in order to draw nearer to Allaah was the Hijrah (migration). This is since it served as a key that opened the door to acts of obedience, a way through which good was achieved, and a path that led towards the abandonment of forbidden deeds.

Then the condition of the Companions, may Allaah be pleased with them, became favorable and their power grew strong. So the migration that was ordained from Makkah to Madeenah came to an end. This is how that unique first generation began - with the Hijrah. Then by the Grace of Allaah, they achieved establishment and victory after that.

However, the Hijrah is not just a period in time that has passed on and come to an end. Rather, it is an act that will remain constant so long as the world exists, continuing to provide us with valuable lessons, important instructions and blessed guidelines.

So due to Hijrah having the high position and status that it has, I decided to write what I could on it, seeking to voice myself through the words of our past scholars and Fuqahaa, by way of their books on Tafseer, Hadeeth and Fiqh. This was so that the conclusive opinion derived can be based on the upholders of knowledge and so that the resulting view can be from its people.

In this study of mine, I talk about the strong relationship between Hijrah and Jihaad. And I dedicated a chapter just for the statements the scholars have made about Hijrah, where they mention the conditions in which it is either obligatory, not obligatory or recommended. The chapter also contains many other important issues.

I also included in this research the extremely beneficial and valuable treatise of (Imaam) Al-Wanshareeshee, may Allaah have mercy on him, bearer of the Maalikee flag during his time, which he devoted specifically to this topic.

And finally, before concluding, I must say:

It is to the benefit of every Muslim in all regions of this world to exert himself in reading the texts related to this subject and to reflect on them, while seeking guidance from the sayings of the past scholars and Fuqahaa of this ummah. Then it should be left up to him to estimate - and he is a witness against his own self, even though he may put forth excuses[1] - between his either remaining in his land or his migrating from it (i.e. Hijrah). Or whether he should move within his region from one district to another or if he should move from the city to the village or from the village to the desert lands, or the opposite of that, searching for the place of living that is best and most favorable for his affairs of this life and the next.

This is all of course, in accordance with the saying of Allaah, the Most High:

لاَ يُكَلِّفُ اللّهُ نَفْسًا إِلاَّ وُسْعَهَا لَهَا مَا كَسَبَتْ وَعَلَيْهَا مَا اكْتَسَبَتْ

"Allaah burdens not a soul with more a responsibility than it can handle. He (man) gets reward for that (good) which he has earned, and he is punished for that (evil) which he has earned." [Surah Al-Baqarah: 286]

He must seek guidance from the sayings of the hard working and sincere scholars, and he must take his Lord into consideration, while glorifying the signs of Allaah. He must look closely at his state of Eemaan, whether it is at a standstill or fluctuating. Is it increasing or decreasing? His heart neither shuts itself off from sins nor does his gaze lower from looking at acts of evil. So to measure one's scale of Eemaan is delicate and to weigh one's balance of Religion is sensitive.

[1] See Surah Al-Qiyaamah: 14-15

I ask Allaah to guide me to the Straight Path and to prevent me from the causes of vain desires and mischief. And I ask Him to accept this deed from me and benefit the Muslim ummah by way of it, making it sincerely and purely for His Noble Face, while not making any part of it for anyone else's sake. Indeed, He is the All-Hearer, the Responder of invocations.

Written by:
Husayn bin 'Awdah Al-'Awaayishah

The Definition of Hijrah

The linguists have noted many uses for the word (*hajara*, to migrate), so I will only mention what will be of benefit to this research, with the will of Allaah.

It is stated in the book *Lisaan-ul-'Arab* (of Ibn Al-Mandhoor):
"*Al-Hajar* (migrating) is the opposite of *al-Wasl* (arriving and establishing oneself). The word Hijrah and *Hujrah* (both) mean leaving from one land to another land. The '*Muhaajireen*' – those that migrated with the Prophet ﷺ – is a derivative of this word. And every person that abandons his place of dwelling transferring to another group of people to live amongst them, he has made Hijrah.

The *Muhaajireen* are called this name because they left their lands and dwelling places, which they grew up in, for the sake of Allaah. And they proceeded until they entered a land, in which they had no family or possessions, which was the case when they migrated to Madeenah. So every individual that separates from his land, whether he lives in the rural areas (i.e. a Bedouin) or in the urban areas, then he is considered a *Muhaajir*. And the noun form derived from that is Hijrah."

In *Mujmal-ul-Lughah* it states:
"'**And a people made Hijrah (migrated) from one land to another**' means that they abandoned the first for the second."

And it states in *al-Qaamoos-ul-Muheet*:
"The phrase '*hajara Hajran*' or '*Hijraanan*' means that one has cut himself off or separated from something or someone. And the noun form of it is Hijrah."

It is stated in *Fat'h-ul-Baaree* (7/229):
"The origin of the word Hijrah comes from migrating from one's homeland."

The following is recorded in *an-Nihaayah* and other books:

"When there occurs the mention of two Hijrahs in a hadeeth, then it refers to the Hijrah made to Abyssinia and the Hijrah made to Madeenah." [2]

[2] Among these ahaadeeth is the statement of the Prophet ﷺ (to Asmaa bint 'Umays): **"But you, the people of the boat, have the reward of two migrations (i.e. to Abyssinia and Madeenah)."** [Reported by Al-Bukhaaree (3876)] **Translator's Note:** This hadeeth is about a dispute between 'Umar ؓ and an Ethiopian woman, Asmaa bint 'Umays, concerning which group had more right to the Prophet ﷺ and to reward – those who migrated to Madeenah or those who had come on a boat from Abyssinia, and later migrated to Madeenah. The Prophet ﷺ clarified that the people of the boat had more right to the Prophet and to reward since they had performed two migrations. Refer to the hadeeth in *Saheeh al-Bukhaaree* (Eng.: vol. 5, no. 539).

Some of the Texts related to Hijrah and Separating from the Lands of Shirk and Disbelievers

[1] Allaah says:

إِنَّ الَّذِينَ تَوَفَّاهُمُ الْمَلآئِكَةُ ظَالِمِي أَنْفُسِهِمْ قَالُوا فِيمَ كُنتُمْ قَالُوا كُنَّا
مُسْتَضْعَفِينَ فِي الأَرْضِ قَالْوَاْ أَلَمْ تَكُنْ أَرْضُ اللّهِ وَاسِعَةً فَتُهَاجِرُواْ فِيهَا
فَأُوْلَـئِكَ مَأْوَاهُمْ جَهَنَّمُ وَسَاءتْ مَصِيرًا . إِلاَّ الْمُسْتَضْعَفِينَ مِنَ الرِّجَالِ
وَالنِّسَاء وَالْوِلْدَانِ لاَ يَسْتَطِيعُونَ حِيلَةً وَلاَ يَهْتَدُونَ سَبِيلاً . فَأُوْلَـئِكَ عَسَى
اللّهُ أَن يَعْفُوَ عَنْهُمْ وَكَانَ اللّهُ عَفُوًّا غَفُورًا . وَمَن يُهَاجِرْ فِي سَبِيلِ اللّهِ يَجِدْ
فِي الأَرْضِ مُرَاغَمًا كَثِيرًا وَسَعَةً وَمَن يَخْرُجْ مِن بَيْتِهِ مُهَاجِرًا إِلَى اللّهِ
وَرَسُولِهِ ثُمَّ يُدْرِكْهُ الْمَوْتُ فَقَدْ وَقَعَ أَجْرُهُ عَلى اللّهِ وَكَانَ اللّهُ غَفُورًا
رَّحِيمًا

"Verily, as for those whom the angels take (in death) while they are wronging themselves (by not performing Hijrah), they (angels) will say (to them): 'In what (condition) were you?' They will reply: 'We were weak and oppressed in the earth.' They (angels) will say: 'Was not the earth of Allaah spacious enough for you to migrate therein?' Such men will find their abode in Hell – what an evil destination! Except the weak ones among men, women and children who cannot devise a plan, nor are they able to find a way (to make Hijrah). These are the ones whom Allaah is (most) likely to forgive, and Allaah is Ever Oft-Pardoning, Most Forgiving. And whoever migrates in the Way of Allaah, he will find many dwelling places and plenty (of sustenance) to live by. And whoever leaves his home as an emigrant unto Allaah and His Messenger, and death overtakes him, his reward is then surely incumbent upon Allaah. And Allaah is Ever Oft-Forgiving, Most Merciful." [Surah An-Nisaa: 97-100]

The following occurs in *Tafseer al-Qurtubee*: [3]
"Ibn Al-'Arabee, may Allaah have mercy on him, said: 'The scholars have divided traveling to different lands into two categories: (1) that which is

[3] *Tafseer Li-Ahkaam-il-Qur'aan* of Imaam Al-Qurtubee (7/350)

done as a result of fleeing and (2) that which is done for the purpose of seeking. The first category is further divided into six types:

1. Hijrah - and that is migrating from a Land of War (*Daar-ul-Harb*)[4] to a Land of the Muslims. This type of Hijrah was obligatory during the Prophet's time and remains obligatory until the Day of Judgement...

2. Leaving from a land of innovation (*bid'ah*).

3. Migrating from a land where the unlawful is dominant and widespread.

4. Fleeing away from that which is harmful to one's body.

5. The fear of getting sick in a land that has an unhealthy atmosphere and leaving from there to a land in which one can walk freely outside (without getting sick).

6. Fleeing for fear that harm will be inflicted upon one's wealth." [5]

Al-Haafidh Ibn Katheer, may Allaah have mercy on him, said in his *Tafseer*: "Ad-Dahhaak said: 'This *ayah* was revealed concerning a group of people among the hypocrites who remained in Makkah instead of going with the Messenger of Allaah (to Madeenah). They ended up fighting alongside the disbelievers on the Day of *Al-Badr* and were destroyed along with those who were destroyed.' Thus this noble *ayah* was revealed, generally applying to everyone that resides amongst the disbelievers, (1) whilst possessing the ability to make Hijrah and (2) not being able to establish his Religion in that land. So (in this case) he is oppressing himself and committing the forbidden.

---

[4] **Translator's Note:** The term *Daar-ul-Harb* (Land of War) is synonymous with the term *Daar-ul-Kufr* (Land of Disbelief) in that they both are lands in which the Muslim is forbidden to take residence in, according to the conditions mentioned in this book. The great scholar 'Alaa-ud-Deen Al-Mardaawee, may Allaah have mercy on him, said: "Hijrah is obligatory upon the one who is not able to openly display his Religion in a Land of War (*Daar-ul-Harb*), without any disagreement. A Land of War is any land in which the laws of the disbelievers are superior." [This statement will be mentioned later in the book]

[5] I am mentioning this quote in summarized form here, but I will mention it in its complete form in the chapter: **"Some of the Statements of the Scholars on Hijrah."**

This is based on the consensus of the scholars, and also on the wording found in this *ayah*, such that He says **'Verily, as for those whom the angels take (in death) while they are wronging themselves'** because of their not performing Hijrah. **'They will say: In what (condition) were you?'** meaning: 'Why did you reside here and not make Hijrah?' Concerning His statement: **'And whoever migrates in the Way of Allaah, he will find many dwelling places and plenty (of sustenance) to live by'**, this is an incitement towards performing Hijrah and separating from the disbelievers." [6]

Imaam Al-Aloosee, may Allaah have mercy on him, said in his tafseer, *Rooh-ul-Ma'aanee,* after quoting Allaah's statement: **"Was not the earth of Allaah spacious enough for you to migrate therein?"**: "Some of the scholars use this *ayah* as evidence for the obligation of performing Hijrah (migration) from the place in which an individual is not capable of establishing his Religion. This is the opinion of Imaam Maalik. Ibn Al-'Arabee has also reported the obligation of making Hijrah from a land that is plague-stricken." [7]

The following occurs in the book *al-'Ibrah mimmaa Jaa'a bil-Ghazwi wash-Shahaadati wal-Hijrah* of Abut-Tayyib Sideeq Hasan [Khaan] Al-Bukhaaree, may Allaah have mercy on him: "This *ayah* can be used as evidence for the obligation of Hijrah on every individual that resides in a Land of Shirk or in a land in which acts of disobedience to Allaah are being openly committed. This is **on the condition** that one has the ability to perform Hijrah and is not from those who are weak, based on the generality that occurs in this *ayah,* even though the cause for the revelation of the *ayah* was specific according to what was stated previously. What is apparent is that there is no distinction between one place and another place nor between one period of time and another period of time." [8]

In the same page, the following also occurs:
"Allaah says: **'And whoever migrates in the Way of Allaah, he will find many dwelling places and plenty (of sustenance) to live by.'** When this *ayah* was revealed, a group of Muslims migrated to the land of Abyssinia, while another group, which included the Messenger of Allaah ﷺ, stayed

[6] *Tafseer al-Qur'aan-ul-Adheem* of Ibn Katheer (1/555)
[7] *Rooh-ul-Ma'aanee* of Imaam Al-Aloosee (5/126)
[8] *Al-'Ibrah mimmaa Jaa'a bil-Ghazwi wash-Shahaadati wal-Hijrah* (pg. 217)

behind. They then performed the Hijrah (migration) to the honorable city of Madeenah, **and at that point Hijrah became obligatory upon every individual that was oppressed and not able to manifest his Religion openly."** [9]

[2] Allaah says:

إِنَّ الَّذِينَ آمَنُوا وَهَاجَرُوا وَجَاهَدُوا بِأَمْوَالِهِمْ وَأَنفُسِهِمْ فِي سَبِيلِ اللَّهِ وَالَّذِينَ آوَوا وَّنَصَرُوا أُوْلَـئِكَ بَعْضُهُمْ أَوْلِيَاء بَعْضٍ وَالَّذِينَ آمَنُوا وَلَمْ يُهَاجِرُوا مَا لَكُم مِّن وَلاَيَتِهِم مِّن شَيْءٍ حَتَّى يُهَاجِرُوا وَإِنِ اسْتَنصَرُوكُمْ فِي الدِّينِ فَعَلَيْكُمُ النَّصْرُ إِلاَّ عَلَى قَوْمٍ بَيْنَكُمْ وَبَيْنَهُم مِّيثَاقٌ وَاللَّهُ بِمَا تَعْمَلُونَ بَصِيرٌ . وَالَّذينَ كَفَرُوا بَعْضُهُمْ أَوْلِيَاء بَعْضٍ إِلاَّ تَفْعَلُوهُ تَكُن فِتْنَةٌ فِي الأَرْضِ وَفَسَادٌ كَبِيرٌ

"Verily, those who believed and migrated (made Hijrah) and strove hard in Jihaad with their wealth and their lives in the Cause of Allaah, as well as those who gave them asylum and help; these are all allies to one another. And as for those who believed but did not migrate, you owe no duty of protection to them until they migrate. But if they seek your help in Religion, it is your duty to help them, except against a people with whom you have a treaty of mutual agreement. And Allaah sees all that you do. And those who disbelieve, they are allies of one another. And if you (Muslims) do not do so, there will be *fitnah* on the earth and great corruption." [Surah Al-Anfaal: 72-73]

Imaam Ash-Shawkaanee, may Allaah have mercy on him, said in his book, *Nayl-ul-Awtaar*: "Al-Khattaabee said: 'Indeed, Hijrah became obligatory when the Prophet ﷺ migrated to Madeenah, (as well as his Companions) to his presence so that they may fight along his side and learn the tenets of their Religion from him. Allaah affirms this in many *ayaat* of the Qur'aan, to the point that He cuts off the trust of alliance between the one who migrates and the one who doesn't migrate, as He says **'And as for those who believed but did not migrate, you owe no duty of protection to them until they migrate.'** So when Makkah was conquered and people from every

---

[9] ibid

tribe began to enter into the fold of Islaam, the obligatory type of Hijrah came to an end while the recommended type remained." [10]

Al-Baghawee, may Allaah have mercy on him, said in *Sharh-us-Sunnah*: "It is possible to combine the texts from another angle, and so his ﷺ statement: **'There is no (more) Hijrah after the Conquest'** would then refer to the 'Hijrah' from Makkah to Madeenah."

Al-Haafidh Ibn Katheer, may Allaah have mercy on him, said in his *Tafseer*: "The meaning of His saying: **'And if you (Muslims) do not do so, there will be *fitnah* on the earth and great corruption'** is: 'You must disassociate yourselves from the disbelievers and make an alliance with the believers. If you fail to do so, *fitnah* will befall the people.' And that (*fitnah*) means confusion and intermingling between the believers and the disbelievers. Then there will result (from that) widespread and overflowing corruption amongst mankind." [11]

Imaam Al-Aloosee, may Allaah have mercy on him, said:
"**'There will be *fitnah* on the earth'** means that great tribulations will occur as a result of that, which consist of differences of opinion, weakness in *Eemaan* and an open manifestation of disbelief. **'Great corruption'** means the (illegal) shedding of blood, based on what has been reported on Al-Hasan. So what is meant is that there will be great corruption in that." [12]

Concerning Allaah's statement: **"Verily, those who believed and migrated (made Hijrah)"**, Al-Aloosee said: "They are the *Muhaajiroon* – those who migrated for the sake of Allaah from their homes in their motherland, leaving them behind for their enemies (to possess)." [13]

[3] Ibn 'Abbaas ﷺ reported that the Messenger of Allaah ﷺ said: **"There is no (more) Hijrah after the Conquest, but instead Jihaad and good**

---

[10] *Nayl-ul-Awtaar* of Imaam Ash-Shawkaanee (8/178)
[11] *Tafseer al-Qur'aan-ul-Adheem* of Ibn Katheer (2/343)
[12] *Rooh-ul-Ma'aanee* of Imaam Al-Aloosee (10/38)
[13] *Rooh-ul-Ma'aanee* (10/37)

intention. And if you should find any disagreement, then flee (away from it)." 14

It is stated in *Tuhfat-ul-Ahwadhee*: "'**There is no (more) Hijrah after the Conquest**' refers to (the Hijrah) made from Makkah. Al-Khattaabee and others said: 'In the initial stages of Islaam, Hijrah (migration) used to be obligatory upon everyone that accepted Islaam, due to the few amount of Muslims that resided in Madeenah and their need to gather together in unity. However, when Allaah opened Makkah for conquest, the people entered the fold of Islaam in multitudes. Thus the obligation of migrating to Madeenah was cancelled while the obligation of Jihaad and good intention continued to remain obligatory upon whoever rose for its occasion or had an enemy attack him.'" 15

It also states: "The wisdom behind the obligation of Hijrah upon the one who accepted Islaam, also, was so that he may be safe from the abuse of his disbelieving relatives. For indeed, they used to torture those from their ranks that had accepted Islaam, until they apostated from their Religion back to theirs. This type of Hijrah continued with the same ruling (i.e. obligatory) in regards to everyone that accepted Islaam while residing in the lands of disbelief and **having the ability** to leave from there.

Concerning the statement: **'But (instead) Jihaad and good intention'**, At-Teebee and others said: 'This amendment requires the ruling that comes after it to contradict what comes before it. What this means is that the Hijrah, which means to withdraw from one's homeland and which was required upon every individual to perform to Madeenah, came to an end, except for the withdrawing that was done for the purpose of making Jihaad, which remained constant, as well as the withdrawing that was done due to righteous intentions, such as fleeing from the Lands of Disbelief, migrating for the sake of seeking knowledge and fleeing away from trials for the sake of one's Religion. The intention is included in all of these things." 16

---

[14] Reported by Al-Bukhaaree (1834) and Muslim (1864) from the hadeeth of Aa'isha ﷺ. This wording is its complete form. However, in *Saheeh Muslim* (1353) from the narration of Ibn 'Abbaas ﷺ, it occurs without the mention of **"after the Conquest."**
[15] *Tuhfat-ul-Ahwadhee Sharh Sunan At-Tirmidhee* of Al-Mubaarakpuree (5/214)
[16] *Tuhfat-ul-Ahwadhee Sharh Sunan At-Tirmidhee* (5/215)

It is stated in *Badhl-ul-Majhood fee Halli Abee Dawood*:
"As for his ﷺ second statement,[17] then its meaning is: 'Migrating from the Lands of Disbelief to the Lands of Islaam will not cease until the Day of Judgement.'" [18]

There also occurs in it as well as elsewhere, the following:
"The following statement is quoted from Al-Khattaabee in *al-Haashiyah*: 'In the first days of Islaam, Hijrah used to be obligatory, then it became recommended. This is based on the statement of Allaah: **'And whoever migrates in the Way of Allaah, he will find many dwelling places and plenty (of sustenance) to live by.'** This *ayah* was revealed after the Prophet had moved his residence to Madeenah and when the disbelievers' abuse of the Muslims (in Makkah) became severe. Thus, they as well were commanded to change their residence and migrate to his presence. This was in order that they may be with him ﷺ, so that they could support one another if matters were to worsen and so that they could acquire knowledge of the aspects of the Religion from him and better understand it. The biggest fear at that time was from the Qurayshi tribe and the enemies amongst the residents of Makkah.

But when Makkah was conquered, this understanding came to an end and the obligation of Hijrah was uplifted, and it returned to being recommended. So there are two types of Hijrah. The one that came to an end was the one that was obligatory and the one that remained was the one that was recommended.'"

[4] Samurah bin Jundub ﷺ reported that the Messenger of Allaah ﷺ said: **"Whoever keeps intimate relations with a disbeliever and resides with him, then he is just like him."** [19]

It is stated in *Nayl-ul-Awtaar*: "There is evidence in this (hadeeth) for the forbiddance of residing with the disbelievers and the obligation of separating away from them." [20]

---

[17] He means by this, the Prophet's saying: **"Hijrah will not cease until repentance ceases (to be accepted)."** Its references will be mentioned later.
[18] *Badhl-ul-Majhood fee Halli Abee Dawood* (11/372)
[19] Reported by Abu Dawood and others, and it is a sound (*hasan*) hadeeth. See *as-Saheehah* (no. 2330)
[20] *Nayl-ul-Awtaar* of Imaam Ash-Shawkaanee (8/177)

[5] Jareer bin 'Abdillaah ﷺ reported that Allaah's Messenger ﷺ said: **"I am free from every Muslim that resides amongst the disbelievers."** They (the Companions) said: "O Messenger of Allaah, why?" He ﷺ said: **"Their two fires should not be visible to one another."** [21]

Ibn Al-Atheer, may Allaah have mercy on him, said in *an-Nihaayah*:
"This means that it is required as well as obligatory upon a Muslim to keep a large distance between his place of residence and the disbeliever's place of residence. The place where he kindles his (household) fire must not be established in a way such that it is visible and apparent to the fire of the disbeliever, since it is the fire that is kindled inside the place of residence (to keep warm). Instead he should establish his home in the land of the Muslims. Indeed, it is only hated for someone to live next to the disbelievers because there is no covenant or trust with them. Due to this, the Muslims are strongly urged to make Hijrah."

And he, may Allaah have mercy on him, also said: "Their two fires differ, for this one calls towards Allaah while the other one calls towards the Devil, so how can they be in agreement?"

[6] Jareer bin 'Abdillaah ﷺ reported: **"I gave the oath of allegiance to the Messenger of Allaah that I would establish the prayer, pay the Zakaat, give sincere advice to every Muslim and disassociate myself from every disbeliever."** [22]

It is stated in the book *al-'Ibrah* [of Sideeq Hasan Khaan]:
"Ibn Hajr Al-Makkee said in his *Fataawaa* regarding Hadeeth: 'This hadeeth's meaning is that it is required for every Muslim to keep his place of residence far away from the places of residence of the disbelievers, meaning those who are at war with the Muslims. He should not establish his home in a place in which, if he sets up a fire (to warm himself), it would be visible and apparent to the fire that they have kindled in their homes (to keep themselves warm). This is because when he (i.e. the Muslim) has his fire face the other fires, it becomes counted as being one amongst them. It has been agreed upon that Hijrah is obligatory, along with certain

[21] Reported by Abu Dawood, At-Tirmidhee and others, and it is an authentic hadeeth. Refer to its verification in *Irwaa-ul-Ghaleel* (1207)
[22] Reported by An-Nasaa'ee and others, and it is an authentic hadeeth. Refer to its verification in *Irwaa-ul-Ghaleel* (5/31)

conditions, from the land that is at war with the Muslims. The source for mentioning the **'two fires'** looking towards each other is a figurative expression derived from the saying: 'My home is looking out towards such and such person's home', meaning it is facing it.

The reason for the relation between the cause and the effect in regards to their residing amongst the disbelievers is due to their adding to their (i.e. the disbelievers') population. Also, if an army were to seek them out, perhaps they would be prevented from aiding them, since they would see the campfires of the Muslims mixed along with their campfires. This is because when the Arabs would encounter an army, they would know their size in number by counting the campfires that they had. An example of this occurred during the Prophet's quest to conquer Makkah, when the disbelievers sent an envoy to see his army, which was in the passageway of the town of Dhahraan.

So when this great warning against the Muslims' taking residence amongst the disbelievers - which prevents Muslims from waging war against them and brings an absence of fear entering into them - was issued, the Prophet ﷺ made himself free of anyone that resided amongst them. This was because it was a cause for their not making Jihaad against them." [23]

It is stated in *al-Haashiyah* of Imaam As-Sindee:
"Accompanying a disbeliever leads towards Shirk, and taking an oath of allegiance to abandon Shirk entails taking an oath to abandon all the things that lead to it. So therefore, the end result of this oath is the abandonment of accompanying a disbeliever, and Allaah knows best." [24]

[7] In another hadeeth, the Prophet ﷺ said: **"Each Muslim is sacred to another Muslim. Two brothers are supporters for one another. Allaah does not accept the deeds of a disbeliever who has accepted Islaam, until he separates from the disbelievers (and goes) to the Muslims."** [25]

[8] Mu'aawiyah ؓ narrated that Allaah's Messenger ﷺ said: **"Hijrah will not cease until repentance ceases (to be accepted). And repentance will**

---

[23] *Al-'Ibrah mimmaa Jaa'a bil-Ghazwi wash-Shahaadati wal-Hijrah* (pg. 266)
[24] *Al-Haashiyah* (7/148)
[25] Reported by An-Nasaa'ee (1/358); Ibn Maajah (no. 2536) reported the second part of it. Its chain of narration is sound (*hasan*) according to *Irwaa-ul-Ghaleel* (no. 1207).

not cease (to be accepted) until the sun rises from the place where it sets (i.e. the west)." [26]

[9] And in another hadeeth, he ﷺ said: **"Hijrah will not come to an end so long as the disbelievers are fought."** [27]

---

[26] Reported by Abu Dawood (no. 2479) and it occurs in *Saheeh Sunan Abee Dawood* (no. 2166). It was also reported by Ad-Daarimee, An-Nasaa'ee in *as-Sunan-ul-Kubraa*, Al-Bayhaqee, Ahmad and others. It is an authentic hadeeth as occurs in *Irwaa-ul-Ghaleel* (no. 1208).

[27] *Saheeh Sunan An-Nasaa'ee* (no. 3889)

What has been Reported Concerning the "Land of Islaam" and the "Land of Disbelief"

The "Land of Islaam" is: The place where the two *Shahaadahs* (declarations of Faith) as well as the establishment of prayer are openly manifested, and where no disbelieving function is exhibited, unless under an agreement or trust (with the Muslim authorities).

It is stated in *as-Sayl-ul-Jaraar*:
"In regard to the open manifestation of the *Shahaadah*, if the commands and prohibitions enforced in that land are in favor of the Muslims, such that the disbelievers living there are not able to exhibit their disbelief, except upon being granted permission to do so by the Muslims, then this is considered a 'Land of Islaam.' The presence of some disbelieving affairs does not change or harm this condition in any way, since these affairs are not being exhibited through the strength or force of the disbelievers. This was the condition present amongst the disbelieving Jews and Christians who were under the protection of the Muslim State in the Islamic cities. However, if these conditions (mentioned above) are reversed, then the land is no longer considered a 'Land of Islaam', but rather it becomes a 'Land of Kufr.'" [28]

The following occurs in the book *al-'Ibrah mimmaa Jaa'a bil-Ghazwi wash-Shahaadati wal-Hijrah*: "The great scholar Muhammad bin Ismaa'eel Al-Ameer, may Allaah have mercy on him, was asked the following question concerning the Land of Disbelief:

'Is it that which is stated in the interpretations of it found in books - that it is a land in which disbelieving affairs are openly manifested without there being any trust or agreement (between subjected disbelievers and dominant Muslims)? If it is that way, then this would mean that such cities as 'Aden and the cities connected to it, are Lands of Kufr. This is in spite of the Muslims consisting of the majority of the population and the Jumu'ah and congregational prayers being established amongst them, since the power lies in the hands of the Europeans. This (question) also applies to those countries similar to that, such as the country of India. So what is the most correct view in your opinion?'

---

[28] *As-Sayl-ul-Jaraar* (4/575) of Imaam Ash-Shawkaanee

He, may Allaah have mercy on him, responded by saying:
'Imaam Al-Mahdee,[29] may Allaah have mercy on him, said in his book *al-Qalaa'id*[30] that the Land of Kufr and the Land of Islaam were both established according to the consensus of the scholars and that differing only arose in their interpretations. The majority of them say, and they are the most correct, that the Land of Islaam is the land in which the two *Shahaadahs* and the prayer are openly manifested and in which no disbelieving affairs are openly demonstrated, even if it is distorted[31] and hidden, except that there is an agreement and an allowance for them do so (by the Muslim authorities). This would be like the Jews' and Christians' manifestation of their religions in the Muslim lands. Abu Haneefah, may Allaah have mercy on him, and others said: Rather, the Land of Islaam is the land in which the two *Shahaadahs* and the prayer are openly manifested, even if disbelieving affairs are displayed there without there being any allowance for it (by the Muslim authorities).'

It is said that the decisive factor that determines who controls a land is power and dominance. So if the power lies in the hands of the disbelievers, whether through the leader or the citizens, then the land is a Land of Kufr. And if the power belongs to the Muslims, then the land is a Land of Islaam. It is also said that the decisive factor lies in the population. Thus if the Muslims are the majority in number in a land, then that land is a Land of Islaam. And if the majority of the population consists of disbelievers, then it is a Land of Kufr.

It is also said: The control lies in the leader, thus if he is a disbeliever, then the land is a Land of Kufr, regardless if all of the subjects are believers. On the other hand, if he is a Muslim, then the land is a Land of Islaam, regardless if all of the subjects are disbelievers. As for the regions (from larger countries), which the Muslims have taken control over and conquered since the conquests of the days of the Ottoman, Umayyad and 'Abbasid rule and so on, then after the statement of Islaam (*Laa Ilaaha Illaa Allaah*) is made manifest there, it becomes a Land of Islaam. This is since the principle for every one of the Islamic regions, after the manifestation of the

---

[29] He is Ahmad bin Yahyaa bin Al-Murtadaa Al-Yamanee who died in 840H.
[30] He means the book "*al-Qalaa'id fee Tas'heeh-il-'Aqaa'id.*"
[31] See Ash-Shawkaanee's refutation of this word "distorted" (*ta'weel*) in *as-Sayl-ul-Jaraar* (4/576).

Shahaadah, is that the Islaam of its remaining inhabitants is based upon certainty and it cannot be uplifted unless there is certainty.

Therefore, when we come to know with a certain and imperative knowledge, by witnessing or hearing that the disbelievers have taken possession of one of the Muslim lands and that they have conquered and subjected its inhabitants, and it is such that the Muslims cannot manifest the statement of Islaam (*Shahaadah*) openly except with the permission of the disbelieving authorities, then it has become a Land of War (*Daar-ul-Harb*), regardless if the prayer continues to be established there." [32]

So it has been clarified for us in what has preceded that most of the statements given by the scholars in distinguishing the "Land of Islaam" from the "Land of Kufr" involve the following factors:

1. The open manifestation of the two *Shahaadahs* and the prayer.
2. The open exhibition of Allaah's commands and prohibitions.
3. The bulk of the dominance, power and population[33] lies with the Muslims.
4. The rule of their (Muslim) leader.
5. A lack of the open exhibition of disbelieving affairs unless there is a pact or agreement for that on the part of the Muslim authorities.

---

[32] *Al-'Ibrah mimmaa Jaa'a bil-Ghazwi wash-Shahaadati wal-Hijrah* (pg. 233)

[33] No consideration should be given to population unless it is strong, dominant and able to manifest the Religion of Allaah.

The Relation between Hijrah and Jihaad

It is essential for us to know that Hijrah, which is done for the sake of Allaah, goes hand in hand with Jihaad, there being no difference between the two. In fact, it is the first stage from the (many) stages of Jihaad. This is because the person that migrates as a result of being harmed by the disbelievers, he will never sit down and stay lazy in the world. Instead, his yearning will be for Jihaad and he will make it his goal to fight in the Cause of Allaah, hoping to gain Allaah's Pleasure.

And whoever reflects on the Book of Allaah will see that there is a close link between the word "Jihaad" and the word "Hijrah." Just look at the following *ayaat*:

إِنَّ الَّذِينَ آمَنُوا وَالَّذِينَ هَاجَرُوا وَجَاهَدُوا فِي سَبِيلِ اللَّهِ أُولَـٰئِكَ يَرْجُونَ رَحْمَتَ اللَّهِ وَاللَّهُ غَفُورٌ رَّحِيمٌ

"Verily those who have believed, and those who *migrated* and *waged* Jihaad in the Cause of Allaah, all of them hope for Allaah's Mercy. And Allaah is Oft-Forgiving, Most Merciful." [Surah Al-Baqarah: 218]

So the association between Hijrah and Jihaad is evidently clear, as there is no separation between the words **"migrated"** and **"waged Jihaad'**, since both are connected to one and the same pronoun (i.e. those). This is since Allaah did not say: "Verily those who have believed, and those who migrated **and those** who waged Jihaad in the Cause of Allaah."

Allaah says:

فَالَّذِينَ هَاجَرُوا وَأُخْرِجُوا مِن دِيَارِهِمْ وَأُوذُوا فِي سَبِيلِي وَقَاتَلُوا وَقُتِلُوا لَأُكَفِّرَنَّ عَنْهُمْ سَيِّئَاتِهِمْ وَلَأُدْخِلَنَّهُمْ جَنَّاتٍ تَجْرِي مِن تَحْتِهَا الْأَنْهَارُ ثَوَابًا مِّن عِندِ اللَّهِ وَاللَّهُ عِندَهُ حُسْنُ الثَّوَابِ

"So those who migrated and were driven out from their homes, suffering harm in My Cause, and who fought and were killed, then verily, I will expiate for them their evil deeds and admit them into Gardens under

which rivers flow (in Paradise) – a reward from Allaah. And with Allaah lies the best of rewards." [Surah Aali 'Imraan: 195]

And He says:

إِنَّ الَّذِينَ آمَنُواْ وَهَاجَرُواْ وَجَاهَدُواْ بِأَمْوَالِهِمْ وَأَنفُسِهِمْ فِي سَبِيلِ اللّهِ وَالَّذِينَ آوَواْ وَّنَصَرُواْ أُوْلَـئِكَ بَعْضُهُمْ أَوْلِيَاء بَعْضٍ وَالَّذِينَ آمَنُواْ وَلَمْ يُهَاجِرُواْ مَا لَكُم مِّن وَلاَيَتِهِم مِّن شَيْءٍ حَتَّى يُهَاجِرُواْ وَإِنِ اسْتَنصَرُوكُمْ فِي الدِّينِ فَعَلَيْكُمُ النَّصْرُ إِلاَّ عَلَى قَوْمٍ بَيْنَكُمْ وَبَيْنَهُم مِّيثَاقٌ وَاللّهُ بِمَا تَعْمَلُونَ بَصِيرٌ

"Verily those who believed and migrated (made Hijrah) and strove hard in Jihaad with their wealth and their lives in the Cause of Allaah, as well as those who gave them asylum and help – they are all allies to one another. And as for those who believed but did not migrate, you owe no duty of protection to them until they migrate. But if they seek help from you in (matters of) Religion, then it is your duty to help them, except against a people with whom you have a treaty of mutual alliance. And Allaah sees all that you do." [Surah Al-Anfaal: 72]

And He says:

وَالَّذِينَ آمَنُواْ وَهَاجَرُواْ وَجَاهَدُواْ فِي سَبِيلِ اللّهِ وَالَّذِينَ آوَواْ وَّنَصَرُواْ أُولَـئِكَ هُمُ الْمُؤْمِنُونَ حَقًّا لَّهُم مَّغْفِرَةٌ وَرِزْقٌ كَرِيمٌ

"And those who believed and migrated and strove hard in Jihaad in the Cause of Allaah, as well as those who gave them asylum and assistance – they are true believers. They will have forgiveness and a generous provision (in Paradise)." [Surah Al-Anfaal: 74]

And He says:

وَالَّذِينَ آمَنُواْ مِن بَعْدُ وَهَاجَرُواْ وَجَاهَدُواْ مَعَكُمْ فَأُوْلَـئِكَ مِنكُمْ وَأُوْلُواْ الأَرْحَامِ بَعْضُهُمْ أَوْلَى بِبَعْضٍ فِي كِتَابِ اللّهِ إِنَّ اللّهَ بِكُلِّ شَيْءٍ عَلِيمٌ

"And those who believed afterwards and migrated and strove hard in Jihaad alongside you, they are all from you. But kindred by blood are nearer to one another (regarding inheritance) in the decree mentioned by Allaah. Verily, Allaah has knowledge of all things." [Surah Al-Anfaal: 75]

And He says:

الَّذِينَ آمَنُوا وَهَاجَرُوا وَجَاهَدُوا فِي سَبِيلِ اللَّهِ بِأَمْوَالِهِمْ وَأَنفُسِهِمْ أَعْظَمُ دَرَجَةً عِندَ اللَّهِ وَأُوْلَئِكَ هُمُ الْفَائِزُونَ

"Those who believed and migrated and fought in Jihaad for the Cause of Allaah, with their wealth and their lives, they have the greatest rank in the sight of Allaah. They are the successful ones." [Surah At-Tawbah: 20]

And Allaah says:

ثُمَّ إِنَّ رَبَّكَ لِلَّذِينَ هَاجَرُوا مِن بَعْدِ مَا فُتِنُوا ثُمَّ جَاهَدُوا وَصَبَرُوا إِنَّ رَبَّكَ مِن بَعْدِهَا لَغَفُورٌ رَّحِيمٌ

"Then verily your Lord - regarding those who migrated after they had been put to trials and thereafter fought in Jihaad and were patient - verily, your Lord afterward is Most Forgiving, Most Merciful." [Surah An-Nahl: 110]

So the foundation (*asl*) is to link the word **"Jihaad"** with **"Hijrah."** And as for the *ayaat* that do not mention the link between Hijrah and Jihaad, then they are very few and they contain a reprimanding and condemnation of those who don't migrate. An example of this is Allaah's statement:

أَلَمْ تَكُنْ أَرْضُ اللَّهِ وَاسِعَةً فَتُهَاجِرُوا فِيهَا

"Was not the earth of Allaah spacious enough for you to migrate therein?" [Surah An-Nisaa: 97]

This individual has not even complied with the smallest of requirements, so is it possible that something greater (such as Jihaad) can be sought from him?

Another example of this is found in Allaah's saying:

فَلاَ تَتَّخِذُوا مِنْهُمْ أَوْلِيَاء حَتَّىَ يُهَاجِرُوا فِي سَبِيلِ اللّهِ

"So do not take any supporters from amongst them until they migrate in the Cause of Allaah." [Surah An-Nisaa: 89]

And His statement:

وَالَّذِينَ آمَنُوا وَلَمْ يُهَاجِرُوا مَا لَكُم مِّن وَلاَيَتِهِم مِّن شَيْءٍ حَتَّى يُهَاجِرُوا

"And as for those who believed but did not migrate, you owe no duty of protection to them until they migrate." [Surah Al-Anfaal: 72]

So is it likely that participation in Jihaad can be sought from one who doesn't migrate?!

In some places, the incitement for performing Hijrah is mentioned only, and so it is not linked to the word "Jihaad." An example of this is found in Allaah's saying:

وَمَن يُهَاجِرْ فِي سَبِيلِ اللّهِ يَجِدْ فِي الأَرْضِ مُرَاغَمًا كَثِيرًا وَسَعَةً

"And whoever migrates in the Way of Allaah, he will find many dwelling places and plenty (of sustenance) to live by." [Surah An-Nisaa: 100]

A majority of these kind of *ayaat* are mentioned in Surah An-Noor because the context of their wordings relate to the one who refuses to make Hijrah. And Allaah knows best.

Also, when the scholars gave the reasons why Hijrah is recommended for an individual that is able to openly demonstrate and practice his Religion whilst not fearing *fitnah,* they mentioned that one of these reasons was so that the Muslims could have larger numbers and so that they could be prepared for Jihaad in the Cause of Allaah.

Furthermore, anyone that wants to research this issue of Hijrah will find the sources in the books of the scholars under the sections concerning Jihaad. And this is only due to the link and close relation between the two.

Some of the Statements of the Scholars on Hijrah

Know, may Allaah have mercy on me and you, that there are many statements of the scholars[34] regarding the obligation of Hijrah on the person that:

1. Has the ability to make Hijrah,
2. Fears from *fitnah* (affliction), and
3. Does not have the ability to openly manifest his Religion amongst the disbelievers.

I will only mention those statements that I am able to. And I will also mention what I can of the statements of those (scholars) who viewed that Hijrah was recommended for the individual that:

1. Has the ability to make Hijrah, but also
2. Has the ability to openly manifest his Religion amongst the disbelievers.

The opinion of the majority of the scholars concerning Hijrah:

The great scholar Abut-Tayyib Sideeq bin Hasan bin 'Alee Al-Husaynee Al-Qinnawjee Al-Bukhaaree (d. 1307H) said in his book *al-'Ibrah*: "Al-Mawza'ee[35] said in *Tayseer-ul-Bayaan*:[36] 'The majority of the scholars have stated that performing Hijrah (migrating) from the Lands of War to the

[34] There are many statements of the scholars on this topic that I have not mentioned here due to my having already mentioned them in the previous chapter: **"Some of the texts related to Hijrah and Separating from the Lands of Shirk and Disbelievers."** However, this does not include the opinion of Ibn Al-'Arabee since I only mentioned it there in abridged form.

[35] This is an ascription to a big village in Yemen named Mawza', which lies on the road to Hajj from 'Aden. He died around 820H. Refer to *al-A'laam* (6/287). In his book *ad-Daw-ul-Laami'* (8/223), As-Sakhaawee described him as "The Imaam, the scholar of Usool." However, in that book his name is mentioned with an "r" (i.e. as Al-Mawra'ee), but in the books *al-A'laam* and *Al-'Ibrah*, it reads with a "z" (i.e. as Al-Mawza'ee).

[36] This refers to the book *Tayseer-ul-Bayaan Li-Ahkaam-il-Qur'aan* of Jamaal-ud-Deen Muhammad bin 'Alee bin 'Abdillaah, better known as Ibn Noor-ud-Deen. He completed it in 808H. Refer to *Eedaah-ul-Maknoon* (1/343). This book is still in manuscript form. The first volume of it is in Basrah and it contains 500 pages. He finished writing it in 808H. Refer to *al-A'laam* of Az-Zirkilee (6/287)

Lands of Islaam is obligatory. This ruling applies to a person that is not able to openly manifest his Religion.

It is not obligatory on a person that is able to do that (i.e. manifest his Religion), whether through his relatives or through the leadership, just as it was permitted for Al-'Abbaas ﷺ [to remain in Makkah]. However, performing Hijrah is much more preferable. This is how the ruling concerning Hijrah is in our time - it is obligatory on an individual that does not have the ability to outwardly manifest his Religion, and it is recommended for someone that does have the ability to outwardly manifest it. Innovations take the same status as disbelief with regard to the obligation or recommendation of performing Hijrah. As for the remaining types of sins, then it is recommended that one perform Hijrah from them. In spite of this, Hijrah is not obligatory upon him for that purpose solely, unless the unlawful threatens to overtake him, for indeed seeking the lawful (*halaal*) is an obligation." [37]

Imaam As-San'aanee said in *Subul-us-Salaam* after mentioning the hadeeth: **"I am free from every Muslim that resides amongst the disbelievers"**: "The hadeeth is evidence for the obligation of making Hijrah (migration) from all of the lands of the disbelievers, **and not just from Makkah**. This is the opinion of the majority of the scholars." [38]

Abu Bakr Muhammad bin 'Abdillaah, better known as Ibn Al-'Arabee (d. 543H), said concerning Hijrah:[39] "It is divided into six categories:

First: Leaving from a Land of War (i.e. Kufr) to a Land of Islaam.

Second: Leaving from a land of innovation. Ibn Al-Qaasim said: 'I heard Imaam Maalik say: **'It is not permissible for anyone to reside in a land**

---

[37] *Al-'Ibrah* (page 233)

[38] *Subul-us-Salaam* (4/79)

[39] From the most significant types of Hijrah is that which is done for the sake of seeking knowledge. How tremendous is what these sincere and hard-working individuals do – and history is filled with this – for indeed they have abandoned their families and relatives, and their homelands and enjoyments, seeking to get nearer to Allaah, Mighty and Sublime, and hastening towards Paradise, the width of which is (like the width of) the heavens and the earth. They wander through foreign lands and traverse deserts and barren areas, bearing hardships and difficulties.

where the *Salaf* (predecessors) are reviled.' This is correct, for if one is not able to change an evil, he must remove himself from it. Allaah says:

وَإِذَا رَأَيْتَ الَّذِينَ يَخُوضُونَ فِي آيَاتِنَا فَأَعْرِضْ عَنْهُمْ حَتَّى يَخُوضُوا فِي حَدِيثٍ غَيْرِهِ وَإِمَّا يُنسِيَنَّكَ الشَّيْطَانُ فَلَا تَقْعُدْ بَعْدَ الذِّكْرَى مَعَ الْقَوْمِ الظَّالِمِينَ

'And when you see those who engage in false conversation concerning Our *ayaat* (by mocking at them), then turn away from them until they change their speech to another topic. But if the Devil causes you to forget, then after remembering, do not sit in the company of those who are wrong-doers.' [Surah Al-An'aam: 68]

I once said to my Shaikh, the ascetic Abu Bakr Al-Fahree: 'Why don't you travel from this land of Egypt to your own country?' So he responded: 'I do not like to enter a land in which ignorance is vastly predominant and intellect is minimal.' I said: 'Then go to Makkah and establish residence in the proximity of Allaah and His Messenger, for I have come to learn that leaving this country is obligatory due to the innovation and unlawful (*Haraam*) that exist in it.' He then said: 'There is much guidance and direction for the people, which lies in my hands in this land, as well as teaching Tawheed, restraining others from deviant beliefs and supplicating to Allaah, the Most High.'

Third: Leaving from a land in which the unlawful is dominant and widespread, for indeed seeking the lawful is obligatory upon every Muslim.

Fourth: Fleeing from those things that are harmful to one's body. This is a bounty from Allaah in which He has given us an allowance. So if a person fears danger for himself by staying in a place, then Allaah has permitted him to leave from it and to flee for his life's sake, in order to free himself from that danger. [40]

---

[40] He uses as a proof for this the fact that both Ibraaheem and Moosaa fled from their lands.

Fifth: Leaving for fear of getting sick in a land that has an unhealthy climate and coming out from there to a land in which one can walk freely outside (without getting sick).

Sixth: Fleeing from a land out of fear of harm being inflicted to one's wealth. Indeed, the sacredness of a Muslim's property is like the sacredness of his blood. And his family is equal in that respect, if not greater." [41]

Ibn Qudaamah Al-Maqdisee (d. 620H), may Allaah have mercy on him, said: "People are divided into three categories with regard to Hijrah:

First: This includes the one who it is obligatory upon and he is the one that has the ability to do it (i.e. perform Hijrah) while not being able to manifest his Religion in that land. Nor is he able to establish the obligatory requisites of his Religion due to his position of being in the midst of the disbelievers. This type of individual is obligated to make Hijrah due to Allaah statement: **'Verily, as for those whom the angels take (in death) while they are wronging themselves, they (angels) will say (to them): In what (condition) were you? They will reply: We were weak and oppressed in the earth. They (angels) will say: Was not the earth of Allaah spacious enough for you to migrate therein? Such men will find their abode in Hell - what an evil destination!'** [Surah An-Nisaa: 97]

The severe threat that is mentioned in this *ayah* is proof for the obligation (of Hijrah). Also, establishing the obligatory aspects of one's Religion is an obligation in itself, for the one who is able to do that. And Hijrah is from the prerequisites of the obligatory and it is that which makes it complete. So whatever is essential for the completion of an obligation becomes itself obligatory.

Second: The one who is not obligated to make Hijrah. This is the one who has difficulty in doing it, whether it is due to a sickness, his being forced to keep his residence, or a weakness, as is the case with women, children and their likes. Hijrah is not obligatory upon these types of individuals due to Allaah's statement: **'Except the weak ones among men, women and children who cannot devise a plan, nor are they able to find a way. These are the ones whom Allaah is (most) likely to forgive, and Allaah is Oft-**

---

[41] *Ahkaam-ul-Qur'aan* (1/484)

Pardoning, Most Forgiving.' [Surah An-Nisaa 98-99] It is not described as being recommended since the person in this category is not able to do it.

Third: The one who is recommended to do it, even though it is not obligatory upon him. He is the one who has the ability to make Hijrah, but yet is also able to outwardly manifest his Religion while establishing his residence in the Land of Kufr. So it is recommended for him (to migrate to the believers), so that he may fight in Jihaad alongside them, add to the Muslim population, and so that he can assist and support them. It is also so that he can free himself from adding to the population of the disbelievers, interacting with them and seeing the evil that occurs amongst them. Hijrah is not obligatory on him due to his ability to establish the obligatory aspects of his Religion without having to migrate. This was the case with Al-'Abbaas ﷺ, the paternal uncle of the Prophet ﷺ, who used to reside in Makkah while he was Muslim." [42]

Imaam Majd-ud-Deen Abul-Barakaat (d. 652H) said in his book *al-Muharrir*: "Migrating from a Land of War (*Daar-ul-Harb*) is recommended for a person that is able to openly display his Religion while residing in a Land of Kufr." [43]

After quoting Allaah's saying: **"And whoever migrates in the Way of Allaah, he will find many dwelling places and plenty (of sustenance) to live by"**, Imaam Muhammad bin Ahmad Al-Ansaaree Al-Qurtubee (d. 671H) said: "Maalik said: 'This *ayah* indicates that it is not (permissible) for anyone to reside in a land in which the Salaf are reviled and in which something other than the truth is practiced.'" [44]

Imaam An-Nawawee (d. 676H), may Allaah have mercy on him, said:
"If it is the case that a Muslim is weak whilst residing in a Land of Kufr and he is not able to outwardly display and exercise his Religion, then it is forbidden for him to take residence there. Rather, he is obligated to migrate to a Land of Islaam. And if he is not able to do so, then he is excused until he attains the ability." [45]

---

[42] *Al-Mughnee* (10/515)
[43] *Al-Muharrir* (2/170)
[44] *Al-Jaami' Li-Ahkaam-il-Qur'aan* (5/348)
[45] *Rawdat-ut-Taalibeen* (10/282)

The following occurs in *Majmoo'-ul-Fataawaa* of Shaikh-ul-Islaam Ibn Taimiyyah (d. 728H), where he, may Allaah have mercy of him, was asked about the land of Maarideen: "Is this a land at war with the Muslims or at peace with them? And is it obligatory for the Muslim who resides there to perform Hijrah from there to a Muslim land or not? If he is obligated to perform Hijrah, yet doesn't and instead assists the enemies of the Muslims with his body and wealth, is he sinning by doing that? Is a person that accuses him of hypocrisy and reviles him sinning or not?"

He, may Allaah have mercy on him, responded by saying:
"All praise is for Allaah. The blood and property of a Muslim are sacred regardless if they reside in Maarideen or elsewhere. Likewise supporting those who are outside the fold of the Religion of Islaam is forbidden, regardless if they are inhabitants of Maarideen or elsewhere. As for the one who resides there, if he has difficulty in establishing the application of his Religion, then he is obligated to make Hijrah from there. And if it is not this way, then it is recommended for him and not obligatory." [46]

Al-Haafidh Ibn Hajr (d. 852H) said in *al-Fat'h* commenting on the hadeeth: **"There is no (more) Hijrah after the Conquest"**:

"So whoever resides there[47] from the Muslims, he falls into either one of the following three categories:

First: He has the ability to migrate from there, and he cannot openly display his Religion or perform his obligatory duties. So making Hijrah from this land is obligatory on him.

Second: He is able to make Hijrah, however, he also has the ability to openly demonstrate his Religion and fulfill his religious obligations. In this case, it is recommended for him to make Hijrah, since he will be increasing the number of Muslims in the land he migrates to, as well as assisting them and enabling himself to make Jihaad against the disbelievers. Likewise, he will be safe from the betrayal and treachery of the disbelievers and he will free himself from seeing the evil that occurs amongst them.

---

[46] *Majmoo'-ul-Fataawaa* (28/240)

[47] Meaning: In a land that has not been conquered by the Muslims.

Third: He doesn't have the ability to make Hijrah. Thus he has an excuse for not migrating. Examples of this category are people such as those who are imprisoned or sick or other than that. In this case, his residing in that land is permitted. And if he encourages and forces himself to leave from there, then he will be rewarded." [48]

The great scholar 'Alaa-ud-Deen Abul-Hasan 'Alee bin Sulaymaan Al-Mardaawee[49] (d. 885H) said: "Hijrah is obligatory on the one who is not able to openly display his Religion in a Land of War, without any disagreement. A Land of War (*Daar-ul-Harb*) is any land in which the laws of the disbelievers are superior. Some scholars, such as the author of *ar-Ri'aayatain* and *al-Hawaayatain,* have added to this by stating that it includes any land that has an oppressive ruler governing it or any land of innovation (*bid'ah*), such as that which contains *Raafidah* and *Mu'tazilah* ideologies. I say that this is what is most correct. This (obligation) is restricted to only the one who has the ability to do it (i.e. perform Hijrah). So if he is able to do it, then Hijrah is obligatory on him." [50]

He then said, commenting on the phrase: "It (i.e. Hijrah) is recommended for the one who has the ability to do it (i.e. openly manifest and practice his Religion in that land)": "This is the opinion that a majority of the scholars adhere to and which has been asserted in the books *al-Hidaayah, al-Mudhahhab, Masbook-udh-Dhahab, al-Khulaasah, al-Mughnee, ash-Sharh, al-Muharrir, al-Wajeez* and other works. It has also been mentioned in the introduction of *al-Furoo'* and other books. In spite of this, Ibn Al-Jawzee said that Hijrah is obligatory on him, and he made it absolute, with no exceptions." [51]

---

[48] *Fat'h-ul-Baaree* (6/190)

[49] Abu Falaah 'Abdul-Hayy Ibn Al-'Imaad Al-Hanbalee, may Allaah have mercy on him, said in his biography of him in *Shadhraat-udh-Dhahab* (7/340) regarding those who died in 885H: "Amongst them (i.e. the deceased) is 'Alaa-ud-Deen, Abul-Hasan 'Alee bin Sulaymaan bin Ahmad bin Muhammad Al-Mardaawee As-Sa'adee, then As-Saalihee, Al-Hanbalee. He was the Shaikh, the Imaam, the great scholar, the verifier, the expert, the prodigy of his time, the Shaikh of the (Hanbalee) *madh'hab*, its leader, rectifier, and reviver. Rather he was a Shaikh-ul-Islaam in the absolute sense and a reformer of the Religion by unanimous agreement."

[50] *Al-Insaaf fee Ma'rifat-ir-Raajihi min al-Khilaaf 'alaa Madh'hab-il-Imaam Ahmad bin Hanbal* (4/121)

[51] ibid

Imaam Jalaal-ud-Deen As-Suyootee (d. 911H) said:
"The ayah (i.e. Surah An-Nisaa: 97) is used as proof for the obligation of making Hijrah from the Land of Disbelief except for those who are not able to do it. Maalik said: 'The ayah necessitates the understanding that whoever is in a country in which the aspects of the Sunnah are transformed, he should leave from that land.'" [52]

The great scholar Al-Munaawee (d. 1031H) mentioned the (above) words of Al-Haafidh Ibn Hajr and agreed with it. And he did not mention any statements that opposed or rejected that. [53]

Imaam Mar'ee bin Yoosuf Al-Karmee (d. 1033H) said in *Daleel-ut-Taalib*: "Hijrah is obligatory upon every individual that is not able to openly display his Religion in a place in which the laws of the disbelievers or misguided innovations are dominant. But if he is able to openly practice and exercise his Religion, then it is (just) recommended." [54]

The great scholar Mansoor bin Yoonus bin Idrees Al-Buhootee (d. 1051H), the legal jurist of the Hanbalee school of thought during his time, said: "Hijrah is obligatory on a person that is not capable of openly demonstrating and exercising his Religion in an area in which the laws of disbelief are dominant and superior, or in which the laws of misguided innovations are dominant, such as that of the *Mu'tazilah*. In this case, Hijrah, which means leaving from that land to go to the land of Islaam and the Sunnah, must be performed. This is due to Allaah's statement: **'Verily, as for those whom the angels take (in death) while they are wronging themselves, they (angels) will say: In what were you? They will reply: We were weak and oppressed in the earth. They (angels) will say: Was not the earth of Allaah spacious enough for you to migrate therein?'**

Also the Prophet ﷺ said: **'I am free from every Muslim that resides amongst the disbelievers. Their two fires should not be visible to one another.'** Abu Dawood and At-Tirmidhee reported this hadeeth and what it means is: That one should not remain in an area filled with wicked sinful people. Hijrah is recommended for the one who has the ability to openly

---

[52] See *al-Ikleel* (pg. 99); **Translator's Note:** This quote was added by the translator as it does not occur in the actual book.
[53] *Fayd-ul-Qadeer* (6/438)
[54] See *Manaar-us-Sabeel Sharh ad-Daleel* (1/271)

display and exercise his Religion, while in the regions of a disbelieving land. This (recommendation) is in order that he may extract himself from adding numbers to the ranks of the disbelievers and so that he can be able to make Jihaad against them." [55]

The great scholar, Imaam Ash-Shawkaanee (d. 1255H), said: "Even if the point of benefit (in this hadeeth) is the obligation of migrating from a Land of Disbelief, it does not mean that this obligation is limited to just a Land of Disbelief. Rather, this obligation of Hijrah is an instituted legislation and an established Sunnah, which is to be implemented whenever evil is openly proclaimed, whenever there is a lack of ability to stand up to enjoin the good and forbid the evil, and whenever there is a lack of people that are able to take away what is in the hands of those who consume the things that Allaah has made unlawful.

So it is an obligation upon the believer to save his soul and flee for the sake of his Religion, if he has the ability to do that. And he must look for a land that is void of the open manifestation of disobedience to Allaah, and (a land) that will result in no evil befalling him. If he cannot find such a place, then he is not able to do any better than what he is able to do. He must, however, enjoin the good and forbid the evil with his hand. And if he cannot do so, then with his tongue and if he cannot do that, then with his heart, as the most truthful of people ﷺ has advised us to do. And if he is able to isolate himself by closing his door and placing a barrier between himself and the evildoers, then this is from the least of matters that is binding upon him." [56]

He, may Allaah have mercy on him, also said: "If the open manifestation of disobedience found in another land is **less** than that which is found in his own land, that land becomes a prospective place for him to make Hijrah to."

Then he commented on the words of Al-Mahdee **"except for a beneficial reason"**, saying: "Its meaning is apparent in that if the **'beneficial reason'** (for refraining from Hijrah) is so that one can benefit a group of Muslims, so that they may remain victorious, such as by his participating in some events of enjoining good and forbidding evil or by his teaching the people the

---

[55] *Sharh Muntahaa al-Iraadaat* (2/94)
[56] *As-Sayl-ul-Jaraar* (4/576) of Imaam Ash-Shawkaanee

characteristics of good. If it is such that these things outweigh the benefit of him making Hijrah and fleeing for the sake of His Religion, then indeed (at that point) he is obligated to abandon Hijrah, in compliance with this legitimate beneficial reason." [57]

Some comments on these last words of Ash-Shawkaanee:

1. Ash-Shawkaanee, in his commentary and compliance with the statement of Al-Mahdee, does not mention that this view applies to **all of the Muslims**, since it is obligatory upon everyone that is not able to openly manifest his Religion amidst the disbelievers to migrate. Rather, what he states here, is directed to a specific group of people and a particular party from amongst the Muslims – i.e. those who possess a strong foundation in the practice of their Religion, their calling (*da'wah*) towards it and their knowledge of its affairs. This is why the conditions of (1) enjoining good and forbidding evil and (2) teaching the characteristics of good were mentioned.

2. These people will naturally serve to assist those that have difficulty in making Hijrah as well as those who are not obligated to migrate.

3. If this (view) is realized by being implemented practically, and not theoretically, then indeed there is soundness to this view with regard to the abandonment of Hijrah. This is contrary to what has been stated by Al-Wanshareeshee, may Allaah have mercy on him, in his essay, which I have included separately in this research, as shall soon follow, by the Will of Allaah.

4. This opinion is **one of the two** views of Ash-Shawkaanee, since he has stated something contradictory to it in *Nayl-ul-Awtaar* while refuting Al-Maawardee's following statement:

"If one is able to openly manifest his Religion in one of the Lands of Disbelief, then this land becomes a 'Land of Islaam' because of that.[58] Thus,

[57] *As-Sayl-ul-Jaraar* (4/577)

[58] Here occurs the distinguishing factor between the Land of Islaam and the Land of Kufr. Al-Maawardee, may Allaah have mercy on him, has placed the ability to openly manifest one's religion as a condition for that, saying: "Then this land becomes a Land of Islaam because of that." So the differing comes to an end with this. One of the ways

taking residence in that land becomes better than leaving it for another, due to what can be anticipated from his causing others to enter into the fold of Islaam."

Ash-Shawkaanee refuted him by saying: "It is quite clear that this opinion contradicts the *ahaadeeth* mentioned in the previous chapter, which indicate the forbiddance of residing in the 'Land of Disbelief.'" [59]

A summary of Ash-Shawkaanee's words:

There is room for *ijtihaad* (further investigation) in this verdict as well as a vast amount of discussion left to the matter. This verdict (*fatwa*) does not apply to every Muslim, but rather to an exclusive group amongst them that consists of members that are strong in their Religion, knowledge, *Da'wah* (Calling), and ability to serve those that are not obligated to make Hijrah or those that are unable to do it. However, when any of these individuals is engulfed by or fears the occurrence of affliction in his Religion, then indeed, he becomes obligated to make Hijrah from the Land of Kufr.

Ash-Shawkaanee, may Allaah have mercy on him, also said:
"**Chapter: The permanence of performing Hijrah from the Land of War to the Land of Islaam:** It has been related in *al-Bahr* that migrating from the Land of Kufr is obligatory, according to the consensus of the scholars. This is such that if it is not done, it would be an encouragement to commit disobedience by doing the unlawful or abandoning the obligatory. The leader (Imaam) can request it in order to strengthen his authority." [60]

---

the scholars have defined the Land of Islaam is that it is: "The land in which the two declarations of Faith and the prayer are manifest, and no aspect of disbelief occurs in it without the permission (of the Muslim authorities)." What is understood from this statement of his is that the Muslims must be many and in power and that disbelief and its people should be fading away. This is how they would manifest their Religion, and due to this the land would become a Land of Islaam. And I don't think anyone will say: "Traveling from the land of Islaam is better than residing in it." This is why the scholars have recommended Hijrah for the one who is able to outwardly manifest his religion in a Land of Kufr, so that he may increase the population of the Muslims and so that he may be prepared for Jihaad in the Cause of Allaah.

[59] *Nayl-ul-Awtaar* (8/178)

[60] *Nayl-ul-Awtaar* (8/179)

Shaikh Abut-Tayyib Sideeq Hasan Al-Bukhaaree (d. 1307H), may Allaah have mercy on him, said: "Shaikh Jamaal Al-Makkee, may Allaah have mercy on him, said in one of his legal rulings: 'Hijrah from a land that a Muslim wants to leave in order to rectify his Religion, i.e. to Makkah or any other Islamic city is everlasting. And the establishment of its ruling is constant up until the end of time, as is indicated in the reports of our distinguished scholars.' Ismaa'eel Al-Haqqee, may Allaah have mercy on him, said in his tafseer, *Rooh-ul-Bayaan*, commenting on Allaah's words: **'Was not the earth of Allaah spacious?'**: 'This noble verse directs towards the obligation of making Hijrah (migration) from a place where one is not able to perform the requirements of his Religion, in whatever way he tries to do so.'

Al-Haraadee said in his *Tafseer*: 'There is evidence in this *ayah*, that no one has an excuse for taking residence in a land filled with disobedience for the sake of his wealth, children or family. Rather, he must withdraw from his homeland if he doesn't possess the ability to manifest the truth there. Due to this, it has been reported on Sa'eed bin Jubair that he said: 'If acts of disobedience are being committed in a land, then leave from it.'" [61]

Abut-Tayyib continued (pg. 240) saying:
"As for the ruling on one who moves to this seized land that has been conquered by the disbelievers, then he is a disobedient evil-doer committing a major sin. This is on the condition that he is not pleased with the disbelief and the laws of disbelief that are present there. However, if he is pleased with them - and we seek Allaah's refuge from that - then he becomes a disbeliever and an apostate. And (all) the rulings concerning an apostate apply to him.

So let the one with common sense reflect: What is the cause that is driving this Muslim to move from a Land of Islaam - which is void of disbelievers - to a land that is controlled by disbelievers, in which they openly manifest their disbelief and coerce all those who reside in it to abide by their laws, which are based on disbelief and *Taaghoot*? What drives them to do this except deviation, a love for this worldly life - which is in fact the main cause for all sins - love for amassing its luxuries without any concern for safeguarding ones religion, a lack of pride at the sight of the degrading of

---

[61] *Al-'Ibrah mimmaa Jaa'a bil-Ghazwi wash-Shahaadati wal-Hijrah* (pg. 239)

Tawheed, and a love for being close to the enemies of Allaah instead of being close to those whom He loves, even though Allaah says: **'So turn away from them...'** And He says:

فَلاَ تَقْعُدْ بَعْدَ الذِّكْرَى مَعَ الْقَوْمِ الظَّالِمِينَ

'So do not sit, after remembering, with people who are evil-doers.' [Surah Al-An'aam: 68]

And He says:

فَلاَ تَقْعُدُوا مَعَهُمْ حَتَّى يَخُوضُوا فِي حَدِيثٍ غَيْرِهِ إِنَّكُمْ إِذًا مِّثْلُهُمْ

'So do not sit with them until they change their topic of speech, (for if you don't) you would then surely be just like them.' [Surah An-Nisaa: 140]

So let him reflect on Allaah's words: **'...you would then surely be just like them.'** This is the consequence of one who is afflicted with being near them. So what do you think is the consequence of the one who takes it upon himself to move to a place that is near them? How can there be any doubt concerning his deviance and the corruption of his Religion. And refuge is sought in Allaah!"

He (i.e. Sideeq Hasan Khaan) said (pg. 250 with abridgement):
"As for a Land of Islaam that has been conquered by the disbelievers, such that it is obligatory upon us to fight them and salvage it from their possession, then anyone that carries goods or foods over to them is being disobedient to Allaah and His Messenger ﷺ, and is committing a major sin. So he should be prevented from doing that. And if he doesn't refrain, then the ruler must punish him, as well as anyone else that holds authority amongst the Muslims. This is even if he has to obstruct and block the road that leads to that land, thus preventing him from going there.

And if this person refuses to stop, it is permissible to restrain his commodities and use it on the road as blockades against the disbelievers, while it remains in the possession of its owner. However, it is not permissible to kill him. Rather, he should be prevented from doing that in the best of manners, which should not lead to causing harm to him. And whoever assists him in that (i.e. trading goods with the disbelievers), then he is his associate in sin, regardless of whether his assistance occurred by way of a saying or an action.

As for the case in which the disbelievers have taken control of a land inhabited by Muslims who are deeply rooted in it by way of their property and children, is their living in this land that has been conquered permissible or not? Are they free from sin, being that they are not content with this and that they hate those disbelievers and hold their remaining in that land as a case of emergency? And is their Eemaan complete or is it deficient, or has it gone away altogether? What about if they are determined to move but do not profess that openly?

What is the ruling on them? And what is the ruling on those who love them, those who hate them, and those who follow their example, when they know full well that what they are doing goes against the Laws of Islaam? What is the ruling on the one who resides there if it is determined that the land's laws are contrary to the Laws of Islaam - rather if it is determined that it holds laws of disbelief? Should he follow the land's laws, be pleased with that and continue to reside there or should he disobey them and migrate from there?

The answer is: That the ruling for this can be known from what we have related to you from the sayings of our scholars, may Allaah have mercy on them. The following is stated in *al-Minhaaj* as well as its explanation *at-Tuhfah*:

'The Muslim who lives in a Land of Kufr, i.e. War, as well as the one in a Land of Islaam, which has (later) been conquered (by the disbelievers) - if he is able to openly exhibit his religion and does not fear any consequences due to his open manifestation of Islaam - it is recommended for him to make Hijrah to the Land of Islaam. The reason for this is so that he won't add to the numbers of the disbelievers, who perhaps may imprison him. Hijrah is not obligatory on him due to his ability to openly manifest his Religion. So in this circumstance, his residing there is not forbidden, since the condition of the Muslim amidst them is only that of subjugation and domination not that of incapacity.

So if he anticipates that he will be able to manifest Islaam by residing there, then his residing there is better. Or if he is able to stay away from the disbelievers, living in seclusion, and doesn't expect that making Hijrah will aid the Muslims, then his residing there becomes obligatory, since his place is (considered) a Land of Islaam. But if he were to migrate, it would become a Land of War. Furthermore, if he is able to fight them and call them to Islaam, he should stay there. If not, he should leave.'

What is apparent is that it is very difficult for this land to turn into a Land of Kufr, even if the disbelievers take over it, as is clearly seen in the authentic report: **'Islaam raises and grants ascendancy, while it is not raised nor granted ascendancy.'** [62]

Concerning their saying: 'Then it would become a Land of War', this means that its outcome would be that way in terms of its appearance and not its ruling. And if he is unable to manifest his religion or fears that he will be put to trial for the sake of his religion, then making Hijrah is obligatory on him - if he is able to do it - and he is being sinful by remaining in that land. But if he is unable to migrate, he is excused due to Allaah's saying:

كُنَّا مُسْتَضْعَفِينَ فِي الأَرْضِ قَالُوَا أَلَمْ تَكُنْ أَرْضُ اللّهِ وَاسِعَةً فَتُهَاجِرُوا فِيهَا فَأُوْلَـئِكَ مَأْوَاهُمْ جَهَنَّمُ وَسَاءتْ مَصِيرًا . إِلاَّ الْمُسْتَضْعَفِينَ مِنَ الرِّجَالِ وَالنِّسَاء وَالْوِلْدَانِ لاَ يَسْتَطِيعُونَ حِيلَةً وَلاَ يَهْتَدُونَ سَبِيلاً . فَأُوْلَـئِكَ عَسَى اللّهُ أَن يَعْفُوَ عَنْهُمْ وَكَانَ اللّهُ عَفُوًّا غَفُورًا

'They will reply: 'We were weak and oppressed in the earth.' They (angels) will say: 'Was not the earth of Allaah spacious enough for you to migrate therein?' Such men will find their abode in Hell - what an evil destination! Except the weak ones among men, women and children who cannot devise a plan, nor are they able to find a way (to make Hijrah). These are the ones whom Allaah is (most) likely to forgive, and Allaah is Ever Oft-Pardoning, Most Forgiving.' [Surah An-Nisaa: 97-98]

---

[62] Reported by Ad-Daaraqutnee in his *Sunan*, Al-Bayhaqee, Muhammad bin Haaroon Ar-Rawayaanee in his *Musnad* and others. It is sound (*hasan*) in itself, as is stated in *Fat'h-ul-Baaree* (3/220), and due to other chains, as is stated in *Irwaa-ul-Ghaleel* (1268).

And it is also due to the authentic report: **'Hijrah will not come to an end so long as the disbelievers are fought.'** [63]

So it is agreed that if the inhabitants of this afore-mentioned land are able to openly manifest their religion and are free from *fitnah* (afflictions), and they do not anticipate that they will assist the Muslims (in any way), Hijrah is recommended for them. And if in that land they are able to withdraw themselves (i.e. to a secluded area away from the disbelievers), and openly manifest their religion and protect themselves,[64] then they are obligated to continue residing there. But if they are unable to openly practice their religion or they fear that their religion will be afflicted by trials, they become obligated to make Hijrah, if they have the ability to do it.

This is the final word with regard to the inhabitants of this afore-mentioned land. What is understood from this is that anyone who is obligated to make Hijrah would be sinning by residing there. As for those who are not obligated to make Hijrah, there is no sin on them for residing there. And whoever is free from sin, his Eemaan remains complete so long as he abides by all of the other requisites of Eemaan. But as for the one who is sinning by residing there, his Eemaan is deficient, even though he may abide by all of the (other) requisites of Eemaan.

It is also understood from this that the loss of one's Eemaan is based on the love and hate in a person's heart. A person that follows their (i.e. the disbelievers') commandments without being forced or subjected to do so is sinful, while one who follows their commandments due to being coerced to do so, but yet hates it in his heart is not sinful. So the ruling on one who is coerced to do something less than disbelief is the same ruling as one who is coerced to commit disbelief.

Yes. Whoever is coerced while having the ability to migrate, is sinning since he is assisting the disbelievers by residing amongst them, and Allaah knows best." [End of Sideeq Hasan Khaan's words]

---

[63] Its references and verification have been mentioned in the Chapter: **"Some of the Texts related to Hijrah."**

[64] One must give special attention to the ability of manifesting one's religion and protecting oneself. So he should have some preparation and strength, which would ward off complete and unequivocal extermination and extinction.

He, may Allaah have mercy on him, also said in the same book (pg. 241 and on): "As for the ruling on raising taxes for this land in order to construct it and erect buildings in it, then the obligation - that is agreed on and based on the religion - with regard to the likes of this conquered land, is that its (Muslim) inhabitants must resist and fight against the disbelievers in that land. And those who reside a short distance away from it, as well as those who exceed that (distance), are required to assist the people of that land in that matter, in a collective and group effort. This is on the condition that the land's inhabitants are not sufficient. So this is the ruling with regard to the likes of this land.

The second quote from *al-Minhaaj* along with its explanation *at-Tuhfah* is: 'Whoever gives way to the disbelievers, allowing them to enter into one of our lands - this is a great matter. So it is required for its inhabitants to defend that land by any possible means that they are able to implement. So if it is possible that they can prepare themselves to fight, then this possibility becomes an obligation for the sake of defending themselves - even upon a poor person, a child, one in debt, a slave and a woman that has strength. And if there is no possibility for them to prepare to fight, then anyone who desires amongst us can defend himself, as a possible solution. This also applies to those who reside a short distance from the land, even if they are not from the people of Jihaad, since they are just like its (that land's) inhabitants with respect to being designated with the obligation of fighting. And those who fall under the previously mentioned distance, as well as those over that distance - if they find provisions, weapons and the means for transportation - are also required to assist according to the extent of a collective obligation. This is if the land's inhabitants and those who are around them are not sufficient enough to defend and save themselves.'

So if the Muslim inhabitants of this afore-mentioned land as well as those who reside a short distance away, in an individual obligation capacity, and those who fall beyond that distance, in a collective obligation capacity, are obligated to fight and resist those disbelievers, liberating the Muslims in it, and extracting the disbelievers from it by way of intense combat, laying siege and impeding, as Allaah commanded in His Book, saying: **'So kill the polytheists wherever you find them and capture them...'**[65] - and this is with regard to the disbelievers when they are in their own lands - then

[65] Surah At-Tawbah: 5

what is the ruling on those disbelievers that have conquered our lands, put us to shame and hurt our honor, except the same? Rather, these individuals take more precedence in this matter.

So whoever departs and readies his boat and riding beast to go to this land, taking goods and products with him to it, bringing to life its marketplaces through trading and its streets through the coming and going of passers-by, constructing buildings in it, and developing its infrastructure, this person has opposed the legislation of Muhammad ﷺ and renounced the divine covenant. And he has become pleased with the laws of the Days of Ignorance:

أَفَغَيْرَ دِينِ اللهِ يَبْغُونَ وَلَهُ أَسْلَمَ مَن فِي السَّمَاوَاتِ وَالأَرْضِ طَوْعًا وَكَرْهًا وَإِلَيْهِ يُرْجَعُونَ

'Do they seek other than the Religion of Allaah, when everyone in the heavens and the earth submits to Him, willingly and unwillingly, and to Him shall they all be returned?' [Surah Aali 'Imraan: 83]

Ibn Sireen was once asked about a man who buys a house from a Christian – is this considered a legitimate business transaction? So he recited Allaah's saying:

وَمَن يَتَوَلَّهُم مِّنكُمْ فَإِنَّهُ مِنْهُمْ

'And whoever amongst you takes them (disbelievers) as allies and protectors, then he is indeed from among them.' [Surah Al-Maa'idah: 51]

So how would you judge the one who supports them by bringing provisions, goods and wealth to them, which only serves to strengthen them and intensify their fighting against Islaam? And what about the one who lowers himself to their might, melting before their tyranny and humbling himself in front of their laws? How, after all this, can he use the names of Eemaan and Islaam for himself when he has submitted himself to the laws of disbelief? Is he seeking honor through them? Verily, all the honor belongs to Allaah! And there is no might or power except by Allaah's Leave.

Allaah says:

يَا أَيُّهَا الَّذِينَ آمَنُوا لاَ تَتَّخِذُوا بِطَانَةً مِّن دُونِكُمْ لاَ يَأْلُونَكُمْ خَبَالاً وَدُّوا مَا عَنِتُّمْ قَدْ بَدَتِ الْبَغْضَاءُ مِنْ أَفْوَاهِهِمْ وَمَا تُخْفِي صُدُورُهُمْ أَكْبَرُ قَدْ بَيَّنَّا لَكُمُ الآيَاتِ إِن كُنتُمْ تَعْقِلُونَ

'O you who believe! Do not take those outside of your Religion as *bitaanah* (helpers/friends), since they will not fail to do their best to corrupt you. They desire to harm you severely. Hatred has already appeared from their mouths, but what they conceal in their hearts is far worse. We have made the *ayaat* (signs/verses) plain to you, if you truly understand.' [Surah Aali 'Imraan: 118]

The word *bitaanah* means outsiders that are made into trusted companions, and it applies to scribes, accountants, gatekeepers and trustees, as well as all the other types that fall under the term *bitaanah*.[66] Afterward, Allaah, the

---

[66] With regard to this topic, 'Umar ﷺ would hate that the *'Ulooj* – who were the males from the non-Arab disbelievers – enter within the Muslim ranks and mix with them, as occurs in *Saheeh al-Bukhaaree* (3700) in the story about his murder, may Allaah be pleased with him: He (this non-Arab disbeliever) had stabbed thirteen men (while they were praying), amongst whom was 'Umar ﷺ. 'Amr bin Maymoon reported: "When they finished praying, 'Umar said: 'O Ibn 'Abbaas! Find out who attacked me.' So Ibn 'Abbaas looked around for a while and came back saying. 'It was the slave of Al-Mugheerah.' So 'Umar asked: 'The craftsman?' Ibn 'Abbaas replied: 'Yes.' 'Umar ﷺ said: 'May Allaah curse him. I did not treat him unjustly. All praise is for Allaah who has not caused me to die at the hands of a man who claims to be a Muslim. You and your father (Al-'Abbaas) used to love that there be many non-Arab disbelievers in Madeenah.' And Al-'Abbaas used to have the greatest number of slaves. So Ibn 'Abbaas said to 'Umar: 'If you wish, I'll do it', meaning 'If you wish, we will kill them.' He ('Umar) replied: 'You are mistaken (for you cannot kill them) after they have spoken your language, prayed towards your Qiblah, and performed Hajj like yours.'"

We understand from this text that 'Umar ﷺ was opposed to the presence of non-Arab disbelievers for fear that dangers would befall the Muslims and harm would be inflicted to their religion, characters and bodies. All of this in spite of them being under the Muslim rule, not to mention the rule of 'Umar ﷺ whom even the devils used to flee from and through whom Allaah closed the doors of *fitnah* (calamity). So when these people begin to speak with our language, pray with our prayer and make Hajj like our Hajj, then we are in danger. And this is in spite of them being under our rule. From the

Most Perfect, gives the reason for forbidding that by stating that they love to put us in hardship and difficulty. Hatred has already become apparent from their mouths, but what they hide in their hearts is far worse. So they should not be given any honor after Allaah has debased them, nor should they be treated intimately, after Allaah has outcast them.

The conclusion derived from the Qur'aan is that we must split away from the disbelievers in all aspects and separate from them in all situations. So there should be no connection between us and them at all.

As for those Muslims in the Lands of Islaam that claim to be from the subjects of the Christian countries, being pleased with that and taking great joy in it, and placing banners on their ships like those of the Christians, which show that they are among their citizens, then these individuals are a people that have become overwhelmed with love for the Christians. They are manifesting the greatness of their dominion and tyrannical rule, assuming that what will establish the world lies in their hands, which is their share of this world and the Hereafter. They limit their sights to just competing for and grasping this world, thinking that the Christians are the most fit and capable of protecting and maintaining it.

If these people are ignorant, and they believe that they are elevating the Religion of Islaam, raising it above all other religions, and that its laws are the most correct laws, while having no esteem for disbelief and its people in their hearts, then they retain the rulings of Islaam (i.e. they are still Muslim). However, they are evil sinners who are committing a great offense, for which they must be reprimanded, disciplined and punished severely.

And whoever lives in a land that is governed by something other than the prophetic laws - if he is required to make something forbidden in the Religion lawful or something lawful in the Religion forbidden - it is not permissible for him to accept that or comply with it. Rather, he must reject that and hold hatred for it, unless he is forced to adhere to these laws under what is known as legal coercion. And if he is governed by something that is

---

most lucid examples of this is their killing of the Khaleefah of the Muslims (i.e. 'Umar). So how much worse would it be if we were to be under their rule and authority, speaking their language, while being tested by their beliefs and dazzled by their culture?!

in accordance with the prophetic legislation, he should accept it out of necessity. But it is not befitting for him to degrade himself by exposing himself to their laws, if he has the ability to make Hijrah. And if this is not so, then this consists of a debasement of the religion and a belittling of Islaam and Muslims. And Allaah says:

وَلَن يَجْعَلَ اللَّهُ لِلْكَافِرِينَ عَلَى الْمُؤْمِنِينَ سَبِيلاً

'And Allaah will never grant the disbelievers a way (to triumph) over the believers.' [Surah An-Nisaa: 141]"

Shaikh Ibraaheem bin Muhammad bin Saalim bin Duwayyaan (d. 1353H) said, explaining Shaikh Mar'ee's comment in *"Manaar-us-Sabeel fee Sharh-id-Daleel"* (1/271): "**'So if he is able to openly manifest his Religion, then it (i.e. Hijrah) becomes optional.'** This means that it is recommended for him to make Hijrah, so that he will be able to make Jihaad and so that he can add to the number of Muslims."

Abul-'Abbaas Ahmad bin Yahyaa bin Muhammad At-Tilimsaanee Al-Wanshareeshee (d. 914H)[67] wrote extensively on this subject. He authored

---

[67] It would have been more proper to place his words after that of Al-Mardaawee, based on the dates of death, but I felt it was better to delay his treatise for last because of its lengthiness.

A Brief Biography of the Author:
He was Ahmad bin Yahyaa bin Muhammad Al-Wanshareeshee At-Tilimsaanee, Abul-'Abbaas, the great scholar and carrier of the banner of the Maalikee *madh'hab* at the head of the ninth century [as stated by Ahmad Baba At-Timbuktee in *Nayl-ul-Ibtihaaj* and mentioned by Husayn Mu'annas in the introduction of his treatise].

He acquired knowledge from the scholars of Tilimsaan, such as Imaam Abul-Fadl Qaasim Al-'Uqbaanee, Imaam Muhammad bin Al-'Abbaas, the scholar and noble speaker, Ibn Marzooq Al-Kafeef, Al-Gharaabilee, Al-Murree and others. He studied under a group amongst the distinguished scholars, and he used to speak the truth, not being deterred by the blame of the blamers, for the sake of Allaah. The ruler (*sultaan*), Abu Thaabit Az-Zayaanee, became angry with him and ordered his house to be ransacked, so he left for Faas. One day when Ahmad Al-Wanshareeshee passed by him in front of the Qarwayeen Central Mosque, Imaam Muhammad bin Ghaazee said: "If a man were to swear to divorce his wife upon the truthfulness of his claim that Abul-'Abbaas Al-Wanshareeshee mastered the *madh'hab* of (Imaam) Maalik, with regard to his great book "*Asnaal-Mutaajir fee Bayaan Ahkaam man ghalaba 'alaa watanihi an-Nasaaraa wa lam Yuhaajir – wa ma yatarattabu 'alayhi minal-'Uqoobaat waz-Zawaajir.*[68]" [69]

The following occurs in this book:

In the Name of Allaah, Most Merciful, Bestower of Mercy. May Allaah send His praises and peace on our teacher, Muhammad ﷺ and his family. I received a letter written to me by the Shaikh, the Faqeeh the noble speaker and righteous, complete, honorable and pure role-model, the just one, Abu

---

its fundamental and subsidiary issues, he would be true in his claim and not have to divorce his wife." He gathered knowledge on various different subjects. However, he would devote himself to only teaching Fiqh, to the point that someone who didn't know him would say: "He doesn't know anything except for this subject."

He was very eloquent in using his tongue and pen, such that those who attended his lessons would say: "If Seebawaih (a famous grammarian) were to attend his gathering, he would take (i.e. learn) the grammar from his tongue." Or it is a statement similar to this. A large number of Fuqahaa were produced through him, who later went on to reach high positions in teaching, judging and issuing rulings.

He authored numerous books, among which are: (1) "*Al-Mi'yaar-ul-Mu'arab wal-Jaami'-ul-Mugharab 'an Fataawaa 'Ulamaa Ifreeqiyah wal-Andalus wal-Maghrib*" in twelve volumes; (2) "*Eedaah-ul-Masaalik ilaa Qawaa'id-il-Imaam Maalik*"; (3) "*Al-Qawaa'id*" concerning Maalikee Fiqh; (4) "*Al-Wilaayaat*" concerning positions in an Islamic government; (5) "*Al-Faarooq*" regarding issues of Fiqh; (6) "*Al-Manhaj-ul-Faa'iq wal-Manhal-ur-Raa'iq fee Ahkaam-il-Wathaa'iq*"; (7) "*Nawaazil-ul-Mi'yaar*"; (8) "*Al-Qasd-ul-Waajib fee Ma'rifat Istilaah Ibn al-Haajib*"; and (9) "*Hill-ur-Rabqah 'an Aseer as-Safqah.*"

Many books contain a biography for him, such as: "*Nayl-ul-Ibtihaaj*"; "*Nafah-ut-Teeb*" of Al-Muqree; "*Fahras-ul-Fahaaris*"; "*Mu'jam-ul-Matboo'aat*"; "*Hadeeyat-ul-'Aarifeen*" and many other books, such as the book "*al-A'laam*" and the introduction of the book "*Al-Mi'yaar-ul-Mu'arab*", from where I took this biography.

[68] I got the title of this book and the supplement that follows after it from the noble brother Mash'hoor Hasan Salmaan, may Allaah preserve him and grant benefit through him. **Translator's Note:** The title can be translated as: "The Most Splendid Merchandise: A Clarification of the Rulings on One who had his Land conquered by the Christians but did not Migrate, and what befalls him from penalties and consequences."

[69] Refer to "*Al-Mi'yaar-ul-Mu'arab wal-Jaami'-ul-Mugharab 'an Fataawaa 'Ulamaa Ifreeqiyah wal-Andalus wal-Maghrib*" (3/119) for this treatise.

'Abdillaah Ibn Qatiyyah, may Allaah extend his eminence and superiority, in which he wrote:

"All praise is for Allaah alone. What is your answer, O teacher of mine - may Allaah be pleased with you and benefit the Muslims through your life - regarding the following incident: A group of people among the inhabitants of Andalus migrated from Andalus,[70] leaving behind their homes, lands, gardens, vineyards, and other types of property, and sacrificing much more than that such as money. They came out from being under the rule of the disbelieving religion, claiming that they were fleeing to Allaah, the Most Perfect, for the sake of their religion, lives, spouses and offspring. Because of this, no money was left in their hands or in the hands of some of them. But they were able to settle themselves in a Land of Islaam, all praise be to Allaah, under obedience to Allaah and His Messenger ﷺ and (under) the rule of Muslim guardianship.

However, these people regretted making Hijrah after having reached the Land of Islaam, and they became annoyed, claiming that they found the condition of living there very difficult for them. And they claimed that in this Land of Islaam - which is this country of Morocco, may Allaah preserve it, safeguard its districts and aid its ruler - they did not find any kindness, ease, or support in regards to means that would help them find different forms of standards of living, on the whole. Nor did they find any proper security with regard to being able to act freely without any restrictions in the districts of that land. Because of these conditions, they made different types of vile statements, indicating their weakness in Religion and a lack of valid certainty in their belief system, revealing that their Hijrah was not done for the sake of Allaah and His Messenger - as they claimed - but rather for a worldly reason, which they expected to quickly receive upon their arrival and which was fed to them by their desires.

So when they didn't find what conformed to their ambitions, they began to belittle and talk poorly about the Land of Islaam and its condition, and they began to curse and revile the things that caused them to make Hijrah. At the same time, they started to praise the Land of Disbelief and its inhabitants while professing their remorse for having left it. It was even

---

[70] **Translator's Note:** This refers to Muslim Spain.

noted from some of them, at times, that while criticizing Hijrah to the Land of Islaam, i.e. this country, may Allaah preserve it, they said: 'Is it to this place that one must migrate to from there? Rather, **this is the place** that one must migrate from to go over there!'

And it was also noted that another amongst them said: 'If one of the members of Costello comes to these regions, we will travel to him and request that he send us back there - i.e. to the Land of Disbelief - and that they allow us to enter under the subjected rule of disbelief, whichever way they can!'

Have they fallen into sin, deficiency in religious standing and harm with regard to this matter?

Are they committing an act of disobedience, which they were fleeing from in the first place, if they persist in these notions and don't repent to Allaah nor recant from them?

What is the status of the one who after arriving at a Land of Islaam returns back to a Land of Disbelief, and refuge is sought in Allaah from that?

Is it obligatory to publicly punish those amongst them that outwardly profess such statements and their likes or not? This would be in order to present them with an admonition and warning regarding that matter. So whoever repents to Allaah, then he is left alone, and it is hoped that his repentance will be accepted. And whoever persists in this, he is to be punished or rejected - and every one of them (who holds these views) is to be left with what he chooses. So whoever Allaah establishes in a Land of Islaam, while being pleased with this, he has his intention and his reward is upon Allaah. And whoever chooses to return to a Land of Disbelief to live under the disbelieving rule, he is left to go to what Allaah is discontent with. And whoever amongst them condemns the Land of Islaam literally or figuratively he should be boycotted and not trusted.

Please clarify for us Allaah's judgement with regard to all of this. And also, is it a condition of Hijrah that no one should migrate unless it is for a guaranteed worldly objective that he will achieve right after arriving and which will happen according to his plan, such that he can free himself forever from the regions of Islaam? Or is this not a condition? Instead are they obligated to migrate from a Land of Disbelief to a Land of Islaam, regardless if they have sweetness or bitterness, vastness or constrictedness and hardship or ease with regard to worldly conditions? Is the only purpose for migrating to protect one's religion, family and children, for example, and to escape from the disbelieving rule to the Muslim rule, to whatever Allaah wills from worldly conditions - whether sweetness or bitterness, confined living or spacious room, and so on? We would like a comprehensive, distinguished, explanatory and sufficient clarification, may Allaah reward you..."

So I responded to him with the following:

All praise is due to Allaah alone and may the praises and peace of Allaah be on our master and guardian Muhammad ﷺ. Here is the answer for what you have asked about, and Allaah, the One free of all defects, is the One who grants success through his Bounty.

Making Hijrah (migration) from a Land of Disbelief to a Land of Islaam is an obligation until the Day of Judgement. This also applies to countries filled with unlawful things and falsehood due to oppression or affliction. The Messenger of Allaah ﷺ said:

"A time will come when the best of a Muslim's property will be sheep, which he will take to the mountaintops and to the places of rain-falls, fleeing for the sake of his religion in order to save it from afflictions."

This was reported by Al-Bukhaaree, *al-Muwatta,*[71] Abu Dawood and An-Nasaa'ee. Ash'hab reported that Maalik said: **"No one should reside in a place in which something other than the truth is practiced."**

It is stated in *al-'Aaridah:*[72]
"If it said: 'What if there can't be found any land except one like that', then I say: 'Let the person choose the land that contains the least sin. For example, if a land has disbelief in it, then a land that has tyranny in it is better than it. Or if there is a land in which there is justice as well as the unlawful, then a land in which there is tyranny and the lawful is better

[71] This is how it occurs in the original text.
[72] He is referring to the book *'Aaridat-ul-Ahwadhee fee Sharh at-Tirmidhee* of Abu Bakr Muhammad Ibn Al-'Arabee.

than it for residing. Or if there is a land in which there are sins with regard to the rights of Allaah, then it is better than a land in which there are sins that are violations against the worshippers.'"

Al-Wanshareeshee held that it is not permissible to reside in a Land of Disbelief except in the condition where one is unable to make Hijrah: [73]

Evidences from the Noble Qur'aan:

This Hijrah, which is an obligation upon those individuals that have had their fortresses and lands conquered by the disbelievers - may Allaah curse them - is not uplifted in any condition or circumstance except in the case where one has difficulty (in leaving), and not because of one's homeland and wealth, since all of these reasons are invalid in the eyes of the Legislation.

Allaah says:

إِلاَّ الْمُسْتَضْعَفِينَ مِنَ الرِّجَالِ وَالنِّسَاء وَالْوِلْدَانِ لاَ يَسْتَطِيعُونَ حِيلَةً وَلاَ يَهْتَدُونَ سَبِيلاً . فَأُوْلَـئِكَ عَسَى اللّهُ أَن يَعْفُوَ عَنْهُمْ وَكَانَ اللّهُ عَفُوًّا غَفُورًا

"Except the weak ones among men, women and children who cannot devise a plan, nor are they able to find a way. These are the ones whom Allaah is (most) likely to forgive, and Allaah is Ever Oft-Pardoning, Most Forgiving." [Surah An-Nisaa: 98-99]

This **"weakness"** for which Allaah will pardon whoever falls under its description is different from the **"weakness"** that is used as an excuse in the first part of the *ayah*. We are referring to the statement of those who oppress themselves: **"We were weak and oppressed in the land."** This is since Allaah will not accept their statement using that as an excuse. This indicates that they had the ability to make Hijrah, through a certain channel but yet didn't.

---

[73] All of these (bolded) section headings were placed by Husayn Mu'annas, the one who verified and distributed this treatise in *Ma'had ad-Diraasaat al-Misriyyah* (vol. 5, 1278H/1957) with some minor omissions and changes.

Instead, Allaah pardons the **"weakness"** of those who are not able to devise a way out or able to guide themselves out (of their predicament), based on His saying: **"These are the ones whom Allaah is (most) likely to forgive."** When the word **"likely"** comes from Allaah, it means that it is binding (upon Him).

So the one mentioned in the first part of the *ayah* who is weak and who will be punished is he who is able to make Hijrah through (at least) one channel, while the one who is weak and who will be forgiven due to his inability is he who is not able to make Hijrah through any channel. So if the one who is afflicted with residing in a land of Disbelief is unable to flee for the sake of his Religion, nor find a way towards leaving, nor can he devise a plan, and nor does he have the ability to do it under any means and circumstance, such that he is, for example, disabled or a prisoner or he is very sick or extremely weak, then in this case, it is anticipated that he will be forgiven. He is just like a person that is coerced to openly profess disbelief. However, he should still hold a firm intention that if had the ability, he would make Hijrah. And he must accompany this (intention) with a firm resolve that if he were to obtain the ability to leave at any time, he would migrate.

As for the person who is able to make Hijrah through any of the means available and through any plan at hand, he is not excused. Rather he is only oppressing himself if he continues to reside there, based on what is contained in the following *ayaat* and *ahaadeeth*:

Allaah, the Most High, says:

يَا أَيُّهَا الَّذِينَ آمَنُوا لَا تَتَّخِذُوا عَدُوِّي وَعَدُوَّكُمْ أَوْلِيَاء تُلْقُونَ إِلَيْهِم بِالْمَوَدَّةِ وَقَدْ كَفَرُوا بِمَا جَاءكُم مِّنَ الْحَقِّ يُخْرِجُونَ الرَّسُولَ وَإِيَّاكُمْ أَن تُؤْمِنُوا بِاللَّهِ رَبِّكُمْ إِن كُنتُمْ خَرَجْتُمْ جِهَادًا فِي سَبِيلِي وَابْتِغَاء مَرْضَاتِي تُسِرُّونَ إِلَيْهِم بِالْمَوَدَّةِ وَأَنَا أَعْلَمُ بِمَا أَخْفَيْتُمْ وَمَا أَعْلَنتُمْ وَمَن يَفْعَلْهُ مِنكُمْ فَقَدْ ضَلَّ سَوَاء السَّبِيلِ

"O you who believe! Take not My enemies and your enemies (i.e. disbelievers) as friends, showing affection towards them, when they have disbelieved in what has come to you of the truth and have driven out the Messenger and yourselves (from your homeland) because you believed in Allaah, your Lord! If you have come forth to strive in My cause and to

seek My good pleasure (then take not these disbelievers as your friends). You show friendship to them in secret but I am All-Aware of what you conceal and what you reveal. And whoever of you (Muslims) does that then indeed he has gone (far) away from the Straight Path." [Surah Al-Mumtahinah: 1]

And Allaah, the Most High, says:

يَا أَيُّهَا الَّذِينَ آمَنُوا لاَ تَتَّخِذُوا بِطَانَةً مِّن دُونِكُمْ لاَ يَأْلُونَكُمْ خَبَالاً وَدُّوا مَا عَنِتُّمْ قَدْ بَدَتِ الْبَغْضَاء مِنْ أَفْوَاهِهِمْ وَمَا تُخْفِي صُدُورُهُمْ أَكْبَرُ قَدْ بَيَّنَّا لَكُمُ الآيَاتِ إِن كُنتُمْ تَعْقِلُونَ

"O you who believe! Do not take those outside of your Religion as *bitaanah* (helpers/friends), since they will not fail to do their best to corrupt you. They desire to harm you severely. Hatred has already appeared from their mouths, but what they conceal in their hearts is far worse. We have made the *ayaat* (signs/verses) plain to you, if you truly understand." [Surah Aali 'Imraan: 118]

And Allaah, the Most High, says:

لاَّ يَتَّخِذِ الْمُؤْمِنُونَ الْكَافِرِينَ أَوْلِيَاء مِن دُوْنِ الْمُؤْمِنِينَ وَمَن يَفْعَلْ ذَلِكَ فَلَيْسَ مِنَ اللّهِ فِي شَيْءٍ إِلاَّ أَن تَتَّقُوا مِنْهُمْ تُقَاةً وَيُحَذِّرُكُمُ اللّهُ نَفْسَهُ وَإِلَى اللّهِ الْمَصِيرُ

"Let not the believers take the disbelievers as supporters instead of the believers. And whoever does that will never be helped by Allaah in any way, except (in the case) when you fear a danger from them. And Allaah warns you against Himself (i.e. His punishment). To Allaah is the final return." [Surah Aali 'Imraan: 28]

[The author then goes on to mention many more *ayaat* concerning not taking the disbelievers as *awliyaa* (guardians and protectors).[74]]

And Allaah says:

---

[74] **Translator's Note:** This was abridged by the author, Husayn Al-'Awaayishah.

إِنَّ الَّذِينَ تَوَفَّاهُمُ الْمَلآئِكَةُ ظَالِمِي أَنْفُسِهِمْ قَالُواْ فِيمَ كُنتُمْ قَالُوا كُنَّا مُسْتَضْعَفِينَ فِي الأَرْضِ قَالْوَاْ أَلَمْ تَكُنْ أَرْضُ اللهِ وَاسِعَةً فَتُهَاجِرُواْ فِيهَا فَأُوْلَـئِكَ مَأْوَاهُمْ جَهَنَّمُ وَسَاءتْ مَصِيرًا . إِلاَّ الْمُسْتَضْعَفِينَ مِنَ الرِّجَالِ وَالنِّسَاء وَالْوِلْدَانِ لاَ يَسْتَطِيعُونَ حِيلَةً وَلاَ يَهْتَدُونَ سَبِيلاً . فَأُوْلَـئِكَ عَسَى اللهُ أَن يَعْفُوَ عَنْهُمْ وَكَانَ اللهُ عَفُوًّا غَفُورًا

"Verily, as for those whom the angels take (in death) while they are wronging themselves (by not performing Hijrah), they (angels) say (to them): 'In what (condition) were you?' They reply: 'We were weak and oppressed in the earth.' They (angels) will say: 'Was not the earth of Allaah spacious enough for you to migrate therein?' Such men will find their abode in Hell - what an evil destination! Except the weak ones among men, women and children who cannot devise a plan, nor are they able to find a way out. These are the ones whom Allaah is (most) likely to forgive, and Allaah is Ever Oft-Pardoning, Most Forgiving." [Surah An-Nisaa: 97-99]

And Allaah says:

تَرَى كَثِيراً مِّنْهُمْ يَتَوَلَّوْنَ الَّذِينَ كَفَرُواْ لَبِئْسَ مَا قَدَّمَتْ لَهُمْ أَنفُسُهُمْ أَن سَخِطَ اللهُ عَلَيْهِمْ وَفِي الْعَذَابِ هُمْ خَالِدُونَ . وَلَوْ كَانُوا يُؤْمِنُونَ بِالله والنَّبِيِّ وَمَا أُنزِلَ إِلَيْهِ مَا اتَّخَذُوهُمْ أَوْلِيَاء وَلَـكِنَّ كَثِيراً مِّنْهُمْ فَاسِقُونَ

"You see many of them taking the disbelievers as their supporters. Evil indeed is what their souls have put forward. For that (reason) Allaah's wrath befell them and in torment will they abide. And had they believed in Allaah and in the Prophet and in what has been revealed to him, never would they have taken them as supporters. But many of them are rebellious." [Surah Al-Maa'idah: 80-81]

The ones who are **"wronging themselves"** in this afore-mentioned *ayah* are those who failed to make Hijrah, even though they had the ability to do it. This is based on what is found in Allaah's saying: **"Was not the earth of Allaah spacious enough for you to migrate therein?"**

So the **"wrong"** that they inflict on themselves is due to their lack of making Hijrah, choosing instead to reside with the disbelievers and add to their numbers.

Allaah's saying "**As for those whom the angels take (in death)**" indicates that the ones who will be rebuked and punished are only those who die while persisting on residing (in a Land of Disbelief). As for one who repents from that and migrates, but then death overcomes him while he is on the road[75] and so the angels take his soul while he was in the process of leaving them (i.e. the disbelievers), it is hoped that his repentance will be accepted and that he did not die as one who wronged himself.

What also indicates this is Allaah's saying:

وَمَن يُهَاجِرْ فِي سَبِيلِ اللَّهِ يَجِدْ فِي الأَرْضِ مُرَاغَمًا كَثِيرًا وَسَعَةً وَمَن يَخْرُجْ مِن بَيْتِهِ مُهَاجِرًا إِلَى اللَّهِ وَرَسُولِهِ ثُمَّ يُدْرِكْهُ الْمَوْتُ فَقَدْ وَقَعَ أَجْرُهُ عَلَى اللَّهِ وَكَانَ اللَّهُ غَفُورًا رَّحِيمًا

"**And whoever migrates in the Way of Allaah, he will find many dwelling places and plenty (of sustenance) to live by. And whoever leaves his home as an emigrant unto Allaah and His Messenger, and death overtakes him, his reward is then surely incumbent upon Allaah, and Allaah is Ever Oft-Forgiving, Most Merciful.**" [Surah An-Nisaa: 100]

So all of these Qur'anic ayaat or most of them, especially Allaah's statement: **"You see many of them taking the disbelievers as their**

[75] It seems as if he is alluding to the story about the man who killed a hundred people and wanted to repent, as occurs in *Saheeh al-Bukhaaree* (no. 3470) and Muslim (no. 2766). There are many benefits found in this hadeeth, such as that which has been mentioned by Al-Haafidh Ibn Hajr (6/517), when he said: "There is proof in this hadeeth for the virtue of moving from a land in which sin overtakes a person, due to what he will experience there for the most part (i.e. sin) – either because he will be reminded of the acts he did before that and tempted by it or because he will be surrounded by those who will assist him in that and encourage him to sin. This is why the last person (he went to) told him: **'Do not return to your land, for it is a land of evil.'** There is an indication in this that a person who repents must separate himself from conditions that he was normally in during times of sin, and that he must move away from all of that and preoccupy himself with something else besides it."

supporters. Evil indeed is what their souls have put forward..." [Surah Al-Maa'idah: 80-81] are texts that indicate the prohibition of taking the disbelievers as allies and supporters.

As for His saying:

يَا أَيُّهَا الَّذِينَ آمَنُوا لاَ تَتَّخِذُوا الْيَهُودَ وَالنَّصَارَى أَوْلِيَاء بَعْضُهُمْ أَوْلِيَاء بَعْضٍ وَمَن يَتَوَلَّهُم مِّنكُمْ فَإِنَّهُ مِنْهُمْ إِنَّ اللّهَ لاَ يَهْدِي الْقَوْمَ الظَّالِمِينَ

"O you who believe! Take not the Jews and the Christians as supporters. They are supporters of one other. And if any amongst you takes them as supporters, then surely he is one of them. Verily, Allaah does not guide a wrong-doing people." [Surah Al-Maa'idah: 51] This *ayah* serves to only further confirm this prohibition.

And this goes the same for Allaah's saying:

يَا أَيُّهَا الَّذِينَ آمَنُوا لاَ تَتَّخِذُوا الَّذِينَ اتَّخَذُوا دِينَكُمْ هُزُوًا وَلَعِبًا مِّنَ الَّذِينَ أُوتُوا الْكِتَابَ مِن قَبْلِكُمْ وَالْكُفَّارَ أَوْلِيَاء وَاتَّقُوا اللّهَ إِن كُنتُم مُّؤْمِنِينَ

"O who you believe! Take not as supporters those who take your Religion as a mockery and joke - from among those who received the Scripture before you (i.e. Jews and Christians) as well as the disbelievers. And fear Allaah if you indeed are true believers." [Surah Al-Maa'idah: 57]

Al-Wanshareeshee held that anyone who permits this type of residing renounces his Religion and breaks away from the unified body of Muslims:

The constant repetition of these *ayaat* bearing this meaning and their occurring in the same manner and arrangement confirms this prohibition and raises the open possibility. This is since if some understanding is presented in the texts and then further asserted by constant repetition, its strength becomes increased without a doubt. So these Qur'aanic texts, prophetic *ahaadeeth* and decisive agreements mutually assist and support this prohibition.

This is why you will not find anyone opposing this prohibited type of residing and this allegiance with disbelievers from among the Muslims who adhere firmly to Allaah's Mighty Book, which falsehood cannot enter whether from before it or behind it - a revelation from the Most Wise, Most Praiseworthy.

So it is a prohibition that is established in the Religion, just like the prohibition of eating the dead carcasses of animals, blood and flesh of swine, the prohibition of killing a person without due right, as well as sins similar to those which are committed by the five faculties of perception that the heads of all of the beliefs and religions have agreed are forbidden. And whoever opposes this today or wishes opposition for those who reside with them and rely on them, thus allowing this type of residing, downplaying its status and taking its ruling lightly, then he has apostated from the Religion and split away from the unified body of Muslims, and put himself before the unanimous consensus, which no one can oppose, thus violating it.

Abul-Waleed, Ibn Rushd, the "Grandfather", held the view that it was forbidden to reside (in the Lands of Disbelief):

Al-Wanshareeshee, may Allaah have mercy on him, continued his response, saying:

In the beginning of the section: **"Chapter: Trading with the Land of War"** found in his (book) *Muqaddimaat,* the head of the scholars of Fiqh, Al-Qaadee Abul-Waleed Ibn Rushd, may Allaah have mercy on him, said: "The obligation of Hijrah is not removed. Rather, Hijrah is continuous and everlasting until the Day of Judgement. According to the unanimous agreement of the Muslims, it is obligatory on one who accepts Islaam while in a Land of War, to not reside in that land where the laws of the polytheists govern him. Instead he must migrate and attach himself to the Land of the Muslims where the laws of Islaam can govern him.

The Messenger of Allaah ﷺ said: **'I am free from every Muslim that resides with the polytheists.'**

However, it is not forbidden for the one who migrates from his homeland to return to it, if it turns into a Land of Eemaan and Islaam, just as it wasn't forbidden for the Companions of Allaah's Messenger to return to Makkah, for those whom Allaah granted the ability to go back there.

So if it is obligatory, based on the Book, the Sunnah and the consensus of the ummah, for anyone who accepts Islaam while in a Land of War to migrate from it and join the Land of the Muslims and not to live with the polytheists and reside amongst them, so that their laws do not govern them, then how can it be allowed for anyone to enter their lands, where their laws on trading and so on will govern him? (Imaam) Maalik considered it disliked for someone to live in a land where the Salaf were reviled, so what about a land in which the Most Merciful (i.e. Allaah) is disbelieved and in which idols are worshipped besides Him?! No one's soul can agree with this except for a Muslim whose faith is diseased." [End of Ibn Rushd's words]

Proofs from the Prophetic Hadeeth:

As for the evidences for the prohibition of this type of residing from the Sunnah, then it is based on what has been reported by At-Tirmidhee that: The Prophet ﷺ dispatched an army to (the area of) Khath'am, and some people there sought refuge in prostration, but were killed hastily. When news of this was conveyed to the Prophet ﷺ, he commanded that they be given half of the blood money, and then said: **"I am free from every Muslim that resides amongst the polytheists."**

They said: "O Messenger of Allaah, why?"

He ﷺ replied: **"Their two fires should not be visible to one another."** [76]

On the same subject, the Prophet ﷺ said: **"Do not live with the polytheists nor have intimate relations with them, for whoever lives with them or has intimate ties with them, then he is among them."** [77]

---

[76] This narration is authentic except for the part where the Prophet ﷺ commanded them to give half the blood-money. This is how it is in *Saheeh Sunan at-Tirmidhee.* Also refer to *Irwaa-ul-Ghaleel* (1207).

[77] With this wording, the hadeeth is weak. However, it is authentic with the wording: **"Whoever has intimate ties with a polytheist and resides with him is just like him."** It has been mentioned previously. Refer to *as-Saheehah* (2/231).

The textual wording in these two hadeeths define the objective such that it becomes clear to everyone who has good eyesight and sound reasoning. Furthermore, they are both reported amongst the authentic narrations of the six Books of Sunnah, which Islaam revolves around.

They said: There is nothing that contradicts these two hadeeths, nothing that abrogates them, nothing that makes them specific and so on. And no one amongst the Muslims opposes what they mandate. This is sufficient for using them as a proof. And this is on top of the fact that they are supported by the texts from the Qur'aan and the principles of the Religion, which in turn bear witness to them.

In Sunan Abee Dawood, Mu'aawiyah ﷺ stated: "I heard the Messenger of Allaah ﷺ say: **'Hijrah will not cease until repentance ceases (to be accepted). And repentance will not cease (to be accepted) until the sun rises from the place where it sets (i.e. the west).'**" [78]

The complaint of some of the emigrants that the Land of Islaam has difficult living conditions is a fraudulent claim and wrong notion, and it is not allowed for anyone to return to the Land of the Christians under any circumstance:

What was mentioned in the question about some of the emigrants feeling remorse and displeasure for having left the land of the disbelievers to go to the land of the Muslims due to what they claim of there being difficult living standards and a lack of sufficient means is a fraudulent claim and a wrong notion, in the eyes of this noble Religion. So no one holds these thoughts, considering them and directing his attention to them, except one who has weak certainty, rather one who lacks intellect and religion.

How can he imagine such a thing, using that as an excuse for removing the (obligation of) migrating from the Land of War? There is ample room in the Land of Islaam, may Allaah raise its rank, for the strong and the weak, as well as the heavy and the light. Allaah has provided spaciousness in these lands. So whoever is afflicted by a threat from the disbelievers or danger from the Christians - with regard to his religion, family and children - should seek refuge in these lands.

---

[78] Its verification was mentioned previously.

This is since even the prominent and high ranking among the Companions, may Allaah be pleased with them, migrated to the land of Abysinnia from Makkah, fleeing for the sake of their Religion from the abuse of the polytheists. And they were a great group and a noble company of individuals, which included: Ja'far bin Abee Taalib, Abu Salamah bin 'Abd-il-Asad, 'Uthmaan bin 'Affaan and Abu 'Ubaydah bin Al-Jarraah. The condition (i.e. means of living) of the land of Abysinnia was not known to them prior (to the Hijrah).

Others also migrated to different areas besides this, abandoning their homelands, wealth, children, and parents who had banished them, fought against them and waged war with them. They did this in order to adhere to their Religion and to reject their worldly life.

So what about one of the worldly matters, which if abandoned, doesn't take away from gains being achieved amidst the Muslims, and which if rejected, doesn't have an effect on the supply of those seeking livelihood?

This is especially the case with this religious region of Morocco - may Allaah protect it, increase it in glory and honor, and reinforce it from its grief and sorrows, internally and on its borders - since it is one of the most fertile of Allaah's lands and most saturated of countries throughout all of its parts, especially the capital of Faas, its sections, quarters and borders.

If a person concurs with this notion and - we seek refuge in Allaah - lacks decisive intellect and an upright view and understanding, then he has established a proof and evidence against his vile and despicable self, by having preferred an insignificant and low worldly gain over a religious deed that will be of benefit in the Hereafter (i.e. Hijrah). What a terrible preference and choice this is. And the one who favors this over that, while acting on it, is a failure and a loser.

Doesn't this person who has been duped in his transaction - by regretting having made Hijrah from a land in which the trinity is professed, the church bell is rung, the Devil is worshipped and the Most Merciful is rejected - know that a person has nothing else but his Religion? This is since in it lies his eternal salvation and prosperity in the Hereafter. So he must sacrifice his precious life, not to mention the majority of his wealth, for the sake of it. Allaah says:

يَا أَيُّهَا الَّذِينَ آمَنُوا لَا تُلْهِكُمْ أَمْوَالُكُمْ وَلَا أَوْلَادُكُمْ عَن ذِكْرِ اللَّهِ وَمَن يَفْعَلْ ذَٰلِكَ فَأُولَٰئِكَ هُمُ الْخَاسِرُونَ

"O you who believe! Do not let your wealth or your children divert you from the Remembrance of Allaah. And whoever does that, then they are the losers." [Surah Al-Munaafiqoon: 9]

His View that the one who resides in the Lands of the Christians is committing a major sin and he will be subjected to severe punishment (in the Hereafter) but will not reside in Hell forever:

This is what is related to them with respect to the rulings in the worldly life. As for with respect to the Hereafter, then the one who dies while having spent his entire life living with and supporting the disbelievers and not having migrated, or he migrated then returned back to the lands of disbelief and persisted upon committing this major sin until he passed away, and we seek refuge in Allaah from this, then that which Ahlus-Sunnah and the majority of the Imaams are upon is that these kinds of people are subject to severe punishment (from Allaah). However, they will not reside eternally in the Hellfire.

The ruling on the one who belittles the Lands of Islaam and prefers the Lands of the Christians is that of disgrace in this life and the next:

As for the statement you quoted from one with inferior intellect and religion, that he said: "Is this the place we should migrate to?" - intending scorn and condescension with that comment, and the statement of the other fool: "If the ruler of Costello comes to these parts, we will travel to him" and other repulsive and disgusting comments, it is not unknown to your esteemed selves what these two statements contain from repugnance in their intended meaning. It is also quite clear what these two individuals that made such statements possess from deficiency. This is since no one makes such a comment or deems such a statement permissible except for one who has fooled himself, lost his senses - we seek refuge in Allaah from this - and wishes to remove those narrations and understandings that have been authentically reported. No one throughout the vast regions of the Muslim world - from where the sun rises to the where it sets - opposes its prohibition, due to some objective that is invalid in the view of the Legislation, and which neither has a head nor a tail.

So these foolish objections do not emanate except from one whose heart has been overtaken by the Devil, who has caused him to forget the sweetness of Faith and his place in it. Whoever commits this and gets entangled in it has hastened for his rotten self the guaranteed disgrace in this life and the Hereafter. However, in spite of this, he is not equal - in terms of disobedience, sin, transgression, abhorrence, repulsiveness, deficiency and deservingness of the highest degree of blame and condemnation - to the one who abandons Hijrah altogether, by aiding the disbelievers and living amongst the foreigners.

The reason for this is due to the fact that the most that can be produced from the statements of these two wretched individuals is that of determination, which is when one becomes resolute and makes up his mind to perform an action, which in this case, these two did not do.

The conclusion of Al-Wanshareeshee's opinion:

This is the last of what has occurred to me to write here as a response to the question that was written and sent to me by the great jurist, noble speaker, and righteous example Abu 'Abdillaah, Ibn Qatiyyah, may Allaah extend his excellence and superiority.

This response should be translated and titled: "The Most Splendid Merchandise: A Clarification of the Rulings on One who had his Land conquered by the Christians but did not Migrate, and what befalls him from Penalties and Consequences."

I ask Allaah to grant benefit by it and to multiply the reward due to it.

This was stated and hand-written by the servant in need of Allaah's forgiveness, the lowly, the Muslim: 'Ubaydullaah Ahmad bin Yahyaa bin Muhammad bin 'Alee Al-Wanshareeshee.

The treatise was completed on Sunday, the 19th of the sacred month of Dhul-Qi'adah, 896H.

A Supplement: Another verdict from Al-Wanshareeshee about a man who sought residence in Andalus (Spain) in order to serve his Muslim brothers, speak on their behalf and argue in their favor: [79]

The legal jurist, Abu 'Abdillaah, who was mentioned previously, also wrote the following to me:

All praise is for Allaah and may His praises and peace be on the Messenger of Allaah ﷺ. What is your response, dear sir (May Allaah be pleased with you and cause the Muslims to benefit from your lifespan) concerning the following incident:

A man from the people of Marbilla[80] who was known for his good standing and practice of the religion refrained from making Hijrah along with the people of his country in order to search for a brother of his who was missing previously, after having fought the enemy in the Land of War. After searching for news of him but not finding any, he lost hope and decided to make Hijrah.

But then another reason (for staying) was presented to him, and that was serving as the voice and assistant of the needy Muslims that were subjugated throughout his land and likewise their neighbors who were in similar conditions to the west of Andalus. So he would speak on their behalf to the Christian rulers, concerning what befell them from the misfortunes of that time. And he would argue in their favor and rescue many of them from grave predicaments, to the point that it would be difficult for many of them if he were taken away from them. In fact, they would not be able to find an equal replacement for him in that field if he were to migrate, and great harm would befall them upon his removal, if they were to lose him.

So is it allowed for him to reside along with them under the rule of the disbelieving faith due to the benefit that will be achieved by his staying there to assist the subjugated Muslims in need, even though he has the ability to migrate whenever he wishes? Or is he not allowed to do this?

---

[79] He mentioned this in the book *al-Mi'yaar-ul-Mu'arab wal-Jaami'-ul-Mugharab 'an Fataawaa 'Ulamaa Ifreeqiyah wal-Andalus wal-Maghrib* right after the first verdict.

[80] Marbilla was a small port in Andalus (present-day Spain) on the coast of the Mediterranean Sea.

Or is there no allowance for any of them to reside there since the laws of disbelief govern them and especially since they have been granted permission to migrate, along with the fact that many of them are able to migrate whenever they please?

Assuming that he is allowed to stay, is it also allowed for him to pray in his garments, according to his ability, since for the most part, they are not free from filth due to his constant intermingling and mixing with the Christians, his movements between them, and his sleeping and residing in their homes in order to serve the subjected Muslims, as we mentioned.

Please clarify for us Allaah's ruling on this matter, may you be rewarded and thanked, if Allaah wills. And may Allaah's immense peace, which your high position is deserving of, mercy and praises be upon you.

So I replied to him with the following:

Al-Wanshareeshee's opinion that it is not permissible since it is not compatible with the honor of Islaam, and that the people who remain in that land are sinners: [81]

All praise is for Allaah, the Most High. This is the response, and Allaah is the One who grants success through His bounty:

Indeed, our Divine Lord, the One, the Irresistible, has placed humiliation and lowliness as iron chains and collars upon the necks of the accursed disbelievers, which they walk around with in the regions and in the major cities and lands. This is to show the honor of Islaam and the nobility of His chosen Prophet ﷺ. So whoever amongst the Muslims - may Allaah protect them and grant them honor - attempts to transfer those iron chains and collars onto his own neck, then he has opposed Allaah and His Messenger and exposed himself to the displeasure of the Almighty, the Compellor, and thus deserves to be thrown with them into the Hellfire. Allaah says:

كَتَبَ اللَّهُ لَأَغْلِبَنَّ أَنَا وَرُسُلِي إِنَّ اللَّهَ قَوِيٌّ عَزِيزٌ

[81] The word used here, *dajan*, refers to those Muslims who continued to reside in lands after the polytheists had conquered them and began to govern them.

"Allaah has decreed: 'Verily! It is I and My Messengers who shall be the victorious. Verily Allaah is the All-Powerful, All-Mighty.'" [Surah Al-Mujaadilah: 21]

So the obligation upon every believer that believes in Allaah and the Last Day is to strive hard in safeguarding the apex of Eemaan by distancing himself and fleeing from residing with the enemies of the Beloved, the Most Merciful. The excuse used by this afore-mentioned noble person for residing, which was the goal of serving as a translator between the disbelievers and the subjected inhabitants of that land, does not free him from the obligation of Hijrah.

And no one should perceive that the problematic characteristics written in the question serve as an opposition against its obligatory ruling except for one who feigns ignorance or one who is truly ignorant possessing a backward disposition and no knowledge of the faculties of the Religion. This is since residing with the disbelievers apart from the subjected inhabitants and minorities is not permissible or allowed for even an hour on any day due to what comes as a result of that from filth, uncleanness and the corruption of the religious and worldly affairs for the extent of one's entire life.

An example (of these types of corruption) is: The objective of the Religion is that the word of Islaam and the testimony of truth must stand out over its opposites and over anything that contradicts it. It must be pure and free from anything that scorns it and free from the appearance of any aspects of disbelief entering it. So their residing under humiliation and lowliness definitely necessitates that this noble, high, and exalted statement (i.e. the *Shahaadah*) be low and not raised high and that it be scorned and not sanctified. This contradiction to the fundamentals and principles of the Religion is sufficient for you and for those who endure and are patient with it for their entire lives without any need or compulsion (for residing there).

Residing under the laws of the Christians prevents the completeness of one's prayers:

Another example is that the perfection of the prayer, which come next after the two *Shahaadahs* (testimonies of Faith) with regard to virtue, greatness, proclamation and manifestation, cannot be achieved or even imagined except through the perfection of one's open manifestation, prominence, freedom from scorn, and respect while in the dwelling places of the disbelievers and the relationships with the evil sinners, which expose one to time-wasting, scorning, mocking and play. Allaah, the Most High, says:

وَإِذَا نَادَيْتُمْ إِلَى الصَّلَاةِ اتَّخَذُوهَا هُزُوًا وَلَعِبًا ذَٰلِكَ بِأَنَّهُمْ قَوْمٌ لَا يَعْقِلُونَ

"And when you proclaim the call to prayer, they (disbelievers) take it as a mockery and fun. That is because they are a people who understand not." [Surah Al-Maa'idah: 58]

This contradiction should also serve as enough proof for you. [82]

It suspends Zakaat:

Another example is giving Zakaat. It is quite clear to those who possess insight and intellect that giving the Zakaat to the Imaam (i.e. Muslim ruler) is from the pillars of Islaam and the rites of mankind.

As for giving it to someone who will use it against the Muslims then it is also well known that this consists of opposition to all of the religious acts of worship.

---

[82] If we were to reflect on this, we would understand why the Prophet forbade us from traveling to the lands of the enemies with the Qur'aan. The reason for it has been reported in *Saheeh Al-Bukhaaree* (2990) and *Saheeh Muslim* (1869). In one of these reports, the Prophet ﷺ stated: **"...for fear that the enemy will obtain it."**

Al-Haafidh Ibn Hajr said in *Fat'h-ul-Baaree* (6/134): "Ibn 'Abdil-Barr said: 'The scholars of Fiqh have unanimously agreed that the military units and small armies, which one fears may easily be conquered, should not travel with the *mus-haf*. They differed with regard to the larger armies, which are secure from danger. Maalik forbade it without exception while Abu Haneefah made a distinction. The view of the Shaafi'ee scholars has settled on the ruling that it is detested regardless if fear (for security) is a factor or not. Some of them held the same view as the Maalikee scholars. This hadeeth can be used as proof for the forbiddance of a disbeliever purchasing a copy of the *mus'haf* due to what was mentioned previously, which is that they would then have access to belittle it. There is no difference of opinion on this. Rather, differing only occurred on whether it was valid after such a transaction already took place and if he should be ordered to relinquish his property or not.'"

It suspends Fasting:

Another example is Fasting in Ramadaan. It is well known that this act is an obligation upon the people as well as purification for their bodies. It is dependent upon the sighting of the crescent in order to determine when it begins and when it ends. A majority of the time, this sighting is only confirmed through someone's testimony, and this testimony is not conveyed except in the presence of the Imaam and the Khaleefahs. So in the circumstance where there is no Imaam, Khaleefah or testimony, the month cannot be determined since its beginning and end will be doubtful, with regard to legislated action.

It prevents Hajj:

Another example of it is making the pilgrimage (Hajj) to the House (Ka'bah). In spite of the obligation of Hajj being removed from them due to their inability to perform it, it is still something they are entrusted with.

It holds people back from making Jihaad:

[Another example of it is Jihaad],[83] since Jihaad is done in order to raise high the word of truth and wipe away disbelief from the foundations of Islamic actions. It is a collective obligation (*fard kifaayah*) upon the community and during times of urgent need, especially in the places of living mentioned in the question, as well as its neighboring vicinities.

Hence, they are perhaps abandoning it without a due necessity that prevents them from it, in the absolute sense. So they are like those who are resolved to abandon it without any necessity. And those resolved to abandon something without a necessity are like those who abandon it intentionally and out of free choice. Perhaps they may even do its opposite, i.e. by assisting their allies (the disbelievers) against the Muslims, either with their bodies or their wealth. So they serve as soldiers alongside the polytheists. This wrongdoing and deviant act is sufficient alone.

This residing detracts from the affair of Islaam and causes one to be immersed in witnessing acts of evil and sin:

---

[83] I added these words in order to keep with the flow of the context [Husayn Mu'annas]

It has been clarified in this report that their Prayer, Fasting, Zakaat, and Jihaad are deficient, that they are not able to raise high the word of Allaah and the testimony of truth, and that they are negligent about bringing honor and glory to it whilst eliminating from it the contempt of the disbelievers and the mocking of the evildoers.

So how can one who is deeply engrossed in his religion hesitate or one who is very pious and fearful (of Allaah) have any doubts concerning the prohibition of this type of residing, especially when it is accompanied by opposition to all of these noble and honorable Islamic fundamentals, and especially when for the most part it consists of worldly debasement, humiliation and lowliness? And this is on top of the fact that it opposes the honor and elevated status that has been conferred to the Muslims, and calls to scorning and wronging the Religion. It also consists of things that make the ears ring with pain, such as debasement, contempt and humiliation.

The Prophet ﷺ said: "**It is not befitting for a Muslim to debase himself.**" [84]

And he ﷺ said: "**The upper hand (the hand that gives) is better than the lower hand (i.e. hand that takes).**" [85]

It also consists of scorning and mocking. No one that possesses a good sense of manhood will endure such things unless it is due to a necessity. It also entails abuse and revilement of one's reputation, and possibly one's body and wealth. And it is quite clear what this consists of from the standpoint of the Sunnah and manliness.

It also entails being engrossed in having to witness acts of evil and being exposed to filthy and unclean garments, not to mention eating unlawful or doubtful foods.

Fear of the Christians breaking their pacts:

It also consists of the fears that may be anticipated from this type of residing, and they are of several types, amongst which are:

---

[84] Reported by At-Tirmidhee, Ibn Maajah, Ahmad and others, and it is an authentic hadeeth, which has been referenced in *as-Saheehah* (no. 613)

[85] Reported by Al-Bukhaaree (1427), Muslim (1034) and others

Fear of the leader (of that land) breaking his pact, and that as a result, one's life, family, children and wealth will fall under their control. It has been reported that 'Umar bin 'Abdil-'Azeez forbade the people from residing in the island of Andalus even though it was a (Muslim-dominated) outpost at that time with well-known merits, and the Muslims had the glory, supremacy, and large numbers in terms of people and equipment. In spite of this, the Khaleefah at the time - the one whose merits, religious qualities, uprightness, and sincerity to his subjects is agreed upon (by the Muslims) - forbade them from that, for fear that they would go astray.

So how much more so for those who throw themselves, their wives and their children with their own hands under the power, supremacy, and large ranks of the disbelievers, relying on them to honor and fulfill their pact with regard to their Religion. We do not accept their testimony with regard to themselves, not to mention when it is with regard to us. So how can we rely on their claim that they will fulfill their end of the agreement when what is expected of them will occur, and when the current situation bears witness to it, according to those who research and investigate news from the different regions of the world.

Fear for one's life, family, children and wealth from their evil-doers:
It also includes fear for one's life, family, children and wealth from their evil-doers, foolish ones, and extremists. This is on the assumption that their politicians and leader have fulfilled their end of the pact. The common practice (of the disbelievers) bears witness to this and history confirms it.

Fear of one being afflicted with regard to his Religion:
It also includes fear of one being afflicted with regard to his Religion. Assuming that the elders who have more intellect are free from afflictions, who will guarantee that afflictions will not befall the youth, foolish ones and weak amongst the women - if the leaders of the enemies and their satanic helpers take control over them?

Fear of fornication and the violation of one's private parts; An indication of what took place with Al-Mu'tamad bin 'Abaad's sister-in-law:

It also entails the fear of fornication and the violation of private parts befalling one.

When will a man who has a chaste wife, pure daughter or another close female relative feel safe from the possibility of one of the enemy dogs and foreign pigs becoming acquainted with her, beguiling her with regard to herself and her Religion, and thus conquering her and she in turn complying with him. And he will interpose between her and her male guardian (*walee*) by causing her to apostate and by testing her with regard to her Religion. This is the same thing that happened to the sister-in-law of Al-Mu'atamad bin 'Abbaad and her children. May Allaah grant us refuge from the afflictions and abuse of the enemies!

Fear of their customs, language and attire influencing those who reside with them, as was the condition of the inhabitants of Avila:

It also entails the fear of their condemnable ways, language, dress code and customs being passed down to those who reside with them for a long number of years, as was the case with the inhabitants of Avila and other cities, since they completely lost the Arabic language. And when the Arabic language is lost altogether, all of the acts of worship associated with it also became lost,[86] not to mention the loss of the verbal acts of worship, in spite of their great number and the greatness of their virtue.

---

[86] The Muslims conquered Avila in 145H (i.e. 762CE) during the days of 'Abdur-Rahmaan Ad-Daakhil and remained ruling it until 250H (i.e. 864CE) during the reign of Ameer Muhammad when Alfonso III, King of Leon, usurped the power from them. Then the Muslims reclaimed it after a short period of time. And they continued to possess it until it was lost at the hands of Alfonso VI, King of Costello and Leon after he had conquered Toledo three years before that, i.e. 481H (1088CE). The majority of the inhabitants of that land at that time were Muslims, so Alfonso sent large numbers of people from Leon, Astoria, Jalisco, and Vasco to go live there, and so they filled that land. And the majority of the inhabitants now became from the Christians. In the meantime, the Muslims population there now became the minority, however, they preserved their identity. Their example was like that of the Muslims living in Segovia. However, these two colonies (i.e. that of Avila and Segovia) lost the Arabic language, such that nothing remained with them except for some words and the illustration of some letters.* The Muslims continued to live in each of these two lands up until the seventeenth century. [End of quote from Husayn Mu'annas]

* The author comments: "This is a clear contradiction to his previous statement: 'they preserved their Muslim identity' since if a nation loses its language, what remains with it from its identity?!"

Fear of them usurping their wealth by imposing heavy taxes and unjust fines:

It also entails the fear of them usurping wealth by imposing heavy taxes and unjust fines, which leads to them completely absorbing the wealth and having the disbelieving taxes encompass it in one shot as is the case in a special emergency situation, or during several intervals of time. And it is possible that these fines may become extended due to some fabricated reason or justification whose validity cannot be investigated nor contested.

And if those being fined are very weak and obviously defenseless, they will surely not protest these taxes out of fear that this will serve as a cause to stir the motives for animosity (against them by the disbelieving authorities). True events that have transpired in this regard serve as witnesses to the reality of this for whoever investigates. In fact, such occurrences like this may have even transpired in the land that this question is about, as well as other lands, on more than one occasion.

A Summary: The Prohibition of Residing in this Land

So it has become established through these evil situations that have actually occurred and which are anticipated to continue to occur that residing in these types of lands is prohibited. This conclusion is also derived based on the dangers that result from these types of unstable residences from various and common angles that all lead to one outcome.

In fact, the Imaams (i.e. scholars) have even applied the ruling on this issue to other factors based on its clear and strong forbiddance, as the Imaam of the Land of Hijrah (i.e. Madeenah), Abu 'Abdillaah Maalik bin Anas, may Allaah be pleased with him, said:

"Verily, the *ayah* (verse) about Hijrah entails that every Muslim should leave from the country in which the aspects of the Sunnah have been changed, and in which something other than the truth is practiced."

This is on top of the fact that one must leave and flee from the lands of the disbelievers and the abodes of the wicked sinners. We seek refuge in Allaah from leaving behind an excess group of people for the Christians, which they will incorporate into their ranks, and who in turn will be pleased with residing amidst the filthy and impure, while glorifying them.

So there is no excuse for the noble person mentioned in the question to reside in the described manner for said purpose. There is no allowance for him or his companions for that which will befall their garments and bodies from filths and impurities, since being pardoned for this is based on the condition that one has a difficult time protecting himself from that. But there is no difficulty involved when one freely chooses to reside with them and to act in opposition to uprightness. And Allaah knows best, and with Him lies the success.

This was written by the one who sends his greetings upon the adherents of *Laa Ilaaha IllaaAllaah* who have asked him, the destitute and lowly servant that is in need of forgiveness and seeks blessings from those who ask him and go to visit him: 'Ubaydullaah Ahmad bin Yahyaa bin Muhammad bin 'Alee Al-Wanshareeshee, may Allaah grant him correctness.

This is the end of Al-Wanshareeshee's words, may Allaah have mercy on him.

Some Arab poems also contain an incitement to perform Hijrah, such as:

The verses of the poet from Andalus, Ibn Al-'Assaal:

"And hasten in your journeys O people of Andalus
For residing there is nothing more than an error
The thread usually wears away from the edges, but yet I see that
The thread of the (Spanish) peninsula is worn away from within
Whoever lives next to Shirk, will not be safe from its consequences
How can one live in the same basket as that which is filled with serpents?" [87]

[87] *Nafah-ut-Teeb* of Al-Muqree (4/352)

A Summary of What has Preceded

The following is clear from what was stated previously:

First: The unanimous agreement of the scholars on the obligation of Hijrah for the one that is able to do it, while at the same time being oppressed in his Religion, such that he is not able to openly practice it and perform its obligatory acts.

Second: The statements of the people of knowledge indicate that Hijrah is recommended for the one who is safe from oppression while at the same time being able to openly practice his Religion.

From among the scholars that have clearly stated that Hijrah is (just) recommended (and not obligatory) for those who are free from oppression and openly able to practice their Religion was:

1. The majority of the scholars as mentioned by Al-Mawza'ee in *Tayseer-ul-Bayaan;*

2. Ibn Qudaamah;

3. Majd-ud-Deen Abul-Barakaat;

4. An-Nawawee as occurs in *al-Minhaaj;* [88]

5. Ibn Taimiyyah;

6. Al-Haafidh Ibn Hajr Al-'Asqalaanee;

7. 'Alaa-ud-Deen Al-Mardaawee in the book *al-Insaaf fee Ma'rifat-ir-Raajih minal-Khilaaf 'alaa Madh'hab-il-Imaam al-Mubajjal Ahmad bin Hanbal* (4/121), where he said:

"This is the opinion that the majority of the scholars adhere to and which has been asserted in the books *al-Hidaayah, al-Mudhahhab, Masbook-udh-*

[88] This was quoted from him by Abut-Tayyib Sideeq bin Hasan Al-Bukhaaree in *al-'Ibrah* as mentioned previously.

Dhahab, al-Khulaasah, al-Mughnee, ash-Sharh, al-Muharrir, al-Wajeez and other works. It has also been mentioned in the introduction of *al-Furoo'* and other books."

8. Ibn Hajr Al-Haytamee, as occurs in *Tuhfat-ul-Muhtaaj;* [89]

9. Al-Munaawee;

10. Mar'ee bin Yoosuf Al-Karmee;

11. Yoonus bin Idrees Al-Buhootee;

12. Ash-Shawkaanee; and

13. Ibraaheem bin Muhammad bin Saalim bin Duwayyaan.

Al-Mahdee, the author of the book *al-Azhaar,* considered it recommended for one to reside in a Land of Disbelief for a valid reason. Ash-Shawkaanee discussed this view in detail. However, this view only applies to a specific group of people that are strong in their Religion, knowledge, and calling to Allaah, who are able to command the good, forbid the evil, and teach the people the good.

As for Al-Wanshareeshee, may Allaah have mercy on him, he has authored an exclusive treatise opposing this view.

Third: The fact that the scholars deemed Hijrah recommended for those who are safe from *fitnah* should be understood in its actual sense, limited scope and non-universal range. So for example, if a man is safe from *fitnah* and is able to perform the obligatory acts, is this also the case with his wife? And is this also the case with his children and parents? Therefore, do not think that a man is lonely and single and that he has no connection to anyone. Rather, look at him and those whom he supports (i.e. his dependents).

It is based on this that you will be able to understand what the great scholar Al-Wanshareeshee is talking about in his beneficial research. And through

[89] This was also quoted from him by the author of *al-'Ibrah* (i.e. Sideeq Hasan Khaan)

this we will also be able to benefit from the statements of the scholars and truly understand them.

Fourth: Some scholars held the view that Hijrah from the Lands of Disbelief is not obligatory on the one who is safe from *fitnah* (i.e. trials and afflictions) and able to openly practice his Religion.

Fifth: Hijrah is not obligatory on one who is unable to do it.

Sixth: I am not aware of any scholar that held the view that the one who fears for his Religion and is unable to perform its obligatory duties is not required to make Hijrah, but rather should remain in the Lands of Disbelief.

Seventh: Hijrah is not just limited to departing from the countries that the polytheists govern. Rather, the scholars have even mentioned that one should make Hijrah from the countries in which the Salaf are reviled and in which innovations and sins are dominant. So there are various types of Hijrah. [90]

Eighth: If a country cannot be found except for one in which something other than the truth is practiced, [then the Muslim should choose the one that contains the least sin in it. So for example, if there exists a country with disbelief in it, then a country that contains just tyranny is better than it. If there is a country in which there is justice but at the same time unlawful things, then a country in which there is injustice but at the same time lawful things is better than it for residing. If there is a country in which there occurs acts of disobedience against Allaah, then that takes more precedence than a country in which there occurs acts of disobedience in the form of injustices against (Allaah's) servants.] [91]

If there is a country in which its rulers conceal their disbelief and secularism, then that is better than a country in which its rulers openly profess that. If there is a country in which its rulers claim to govern by the laws of Allaah, then that is better than a country in which its rulers reject that. If there is a country in which very, very few of Allaah's laws are

---

[90] Ibn Al-'Arabee's words on this topic have been quoted previously under the chapter: **"Some of the Statements of the Scholars on Hijrah."**

[91] What occurs between the brackets is from the words of Al-Wanshareeshee, may Allaah have mercy on him, in *Asnaal-Mutaajir*, as previously quoted.

implemented but in which some of the etiquettes of Islaam still can be found, then that is better than a country that is governed by the Jews or the Christians. A country in which there are masaajid and Qur'an centers is better than a country in which there are many churches, synagogues, and disbelieving and pagan places of worship.

Does the Hadeeth: "There is no (more) Hijrah After the Conquest" Abrogate the Texts that Obligate Hijrah?

1. In order to find out the answer to this question, we must first produce the Qur'anic *ayaat* that deal with this issue. Among them is Allaah's saying:

إِنَّ الَّذِينَ تَوَفَّاهُمُ الْمَلآئِكَةُ ظَالِمِي أَنْفُسِهِمْ قَالُوا فِيمَ كُنتُمْ قَالُوا كُنَّا مُسْتَضْعَفِينَ فِي الأَرْضِ قَالْوَا أَلَمْ تَكُنْ أَرْضُ اللهِ وَاسِعَةً فَتُهَاجِرُوا فِيهَا فَأُوْلَـئِكَ مَأْوَاهُمْ جَهَنَّمُ وَسَاءتْ مَصِيرًا

"Verily, as for those whom the angels take (in death) while they are wronging themselves (by not performing Hijrah), they (angels) say (to them): 'In what (condition) were you?' They reply: 'We were weak and oppressed in the earth.' They (angels) will say: 'Was not the earth of Allaah spacious enough for you to migrate therein?' Such men will find their abode in Hell - what an evil destination!" [Surah An-Nisaa: 97]

Is there a lack of **"weak and oppressed"** people on earth today? And are people secure in their Religion in all parts of the world?

2. The meaning of the hadeeth: **"There is no (more) Hijrah after the Conquest"** is made clear in what has been reported in *Saheeh Al-Bukhaaree* (no. 3900) on the authority of 'Ataa bin Abee Rabaah, who said: "'Ubayd bin 'Umar Al-Laythee and I once visited 'Aa'ishah ﵂, and we asked her about Hijrah. So she responded: **'There is no (more) Hijrah after today.**[92] **Each of the believers would flee for the sake of his Religion to Allaah and His Messenger ﷺ, for fear that they would be afflicted because of it. But as for today, Allaah has made Islaam manifest and today the servant worships his Lord wherever he wishes. However, there still remains Jihaad and (good) intention.'"**

Al-Haafidh Ibn Hajr said: "His saying: 'We asked her about Hijrah' refers to the Hijrah that was obligatory to Madeenah prior to the Conquest (of

[92] In one narration it reads: **"Hijrah came to an end from the time that Allaah opened up Makkah to His Prophet (for conquest)."** Refer to the abridgement of *Saheeh Al-Bukhaaree* (2/551, no. 1658)

Makkah), which was then abrogated by the Prophet's saying: **'There is no (more) Hijrah after the Conquest.'"** [93]

'Aa'ishah ﷺ responded by saying **"There is no (more) Hijrah after today."** What is meant by the word **"today"** and what does it entail? Were their days like our days in terms of strength and power? For if it were like that, then Hijrah would be terminated for us also.

What makes this clear is her saying: **"Each of the believers would flee for the sake of his Religion to Allaah and His Messenger ﷺ for fear that they would be afflicted because of it. But as for today, Allaah has made Islaam manifest and today the servant worships his Lord wherever he wishes. However, there still remains Jihaad and (good) intention."**

So look at her ﷺ saying: **"But as for today, Allaah has made Islaam manifest."** Why would there be a need for Hijrah from a land in which Allaah has made the Religion manifest and in which He has established the rites of Hajj and 'Umrah and granted the Muslims the incentive of Tawaaf, not to mention the reward found in that. He also multiplied for them the reward for praying in Al-Masjid-ul-Haraam. This also goes for all of the other virtues and special qualities (He placed in Makkah).

Then she said: "And today the servant worships his Lord wherever he wishes." So if our condition was like their condition, such that we could worship Allaah wherever we wish, then Hijrah would be terminated for us.

Al-Haafidh (Ibn Hajr) said: "In her statement: **'Each of the believers would flee for the sake of his Religion'...'**, 'Aa'ishah ﷺ indicates the reason why Hijrah was legislated, and that was due to the fear of *fitnah* (i.e. trials and afflictions). The ruling on a matter goes hand in hand with its cause. So this necessitates the understanding that anyone who has the ability to worship Allaah in any place he wishes is not obligated to make Hijrah.

But if this is not the case, then it is obligatory (for him to migrate). Based on this, Al-Maawardee said: 'If one is able to openly manifest his Religion in one of the Lands of Disbelief, then this land becomes a 'Land of Islaam' because of that. Thus, taking residence in that land becomes better than

---

[93] ***Fat'h-ul-Baaree*** **(7/229)**

leaving it for another, due to what can be anticipated from his causing others to enter into the fold of Islaam.'" [94]

Al-Haafidh Ibn Hajr, may Allaah have mercy on him, also said in *Fat'h-ul-Baaree* (7/229): "Ibn 'Umar ﷺ expressed this understanding clearly in a report transmitted by Al-Ismaa'eelee with the wording: 'Hijrah to the Messenger of Allaah ﷺ came to an end after the Conquest (of Makkah). But the (general) Hijrah will not come to an end so long as the disbelievers are fought.'"

3. The phrase **"after the Conquest"** is an indication of might, power and strength. So any land that the Muslims conquer and it becomes governed with the laws of Allaah, Mighty and Sublime, it is not necessary to look to migrate from it.

4. What further confirms the absence of an abrogation (of the command to make Hijrah) is his ﷺ saying: **"Hijrah will not cease until repentance ceases. And repentance will not cease until the sun rises from its place of setting."** And also his ﷺ saying: **"Hijrah will not come to an end so long as the disbelievers are fought."**

This is what is in conformity with the true reality the Muslims live in during any time and place. Hence, so long as disbelief has strength and power and a Muslim fears *fitnah* (i.e. trials and afflictions) for his Religion and is unable to establish acts of obedience to Allaah, can it honestly be said to him that he should remain in the Lands of Disbelief due to the Prophet's saying: **"There is no (more) Hijrah after the Conquest?!"**

The meaning of the hadeeth has already been stated in what was quoted from *Tuhfat-ul-Ahwadhee* (5/214) and other books, which was:

"**'There is no (more) Hijrah after the Conquest'** refers to (the Hijrah) made from Makkah. Al-Khattaabee and others said: 'In the initial stages of Islaam, Hijrah (migration) used to be obligatory upon everyone that accepted Islaam, due to the few amount of Muslims that resided in Madeenah and their need to gather together in unity. However, when Allaah opened Makkah for conquest, the people entered the fold of Islaam in multitudes. Thus the obligation of migrating to Madeenah was cancelled

---

[94] *Fat'h-ul-Baaree* (7/229)

and the obligation of Jihaad and good intention remained obligatory upon whoever rose for its occasion or had an enemy attack him.'"

It also states: "The wisdom behind the obligation of Hijrah upon the one who accepted Islaam, also, was so that he may be safe from the abuse of his disbelieving relatives. For indeed, they used to torture those from their ranks that had accepted Islaam until they apostated from their Religion back to theirs.

This type of Hijrah continued with the same ruling (i.e. obligatory) in regards to everyone that accepted Islaam while residing in the lands of disbelief and having the ability to leave from there.

Concerning the statement: **'But (instead) Jihaad and good intention'**, At-Teebee and others said: This amendment requires the ruling that comes after it to contradict what comes before it. What this means is that the Hijrah, which means to withdraw from one's homeland and which was required upon every individual to perform to Madeenah, came to an end, except for the withdrawing that was done for the purpose of making Jihaad, which remained constant, as well as the withdrawing that was done due to righteous intentions, such as fleeing from the Lands of Disbelief, migrating for the sake of seeking knowledge and fleeing away from trials for the sake of one's Religion. The intention is included in all of these things." [95]

Al-Baghawee's saying in *Sharh-us-Sunnah* has also been quoted previously, in which he said: "It is possible to combine the texts from another angle, and so his ﷺ statement: **'There is no (more)** Hijrah **after the Conquest'** would then refer to the 'Hijrah' from Makkah to Madeenah."

Al-Haafidh Ibn Hajr mentioned this statement (of Al-Baghawee) in his book *Fat'h-ul-Baaree* (7/229).

Similarly, An-Nawawee said in *Riyaad-us-Saaliheen*: "It means that there is no (more) migrating from Makkah since it had become a Land of Islaam." [96]

---

[95] *Tuhfat-ul-Ahwadhee Sharh Sunan at-Tirmidhee* (5/215)
[96] Refer to the chapter on "Sincerity and Intention"

Al-Munaawee said in *Fayd-ul-Qadeer* (6/438, under no. 9927): "'**There is no (more) Hijrah after the Conquest.'** This is since it had become a Land of Islaam, and Hijrah only applies to the Lands of War (i.e. Disbelief). So this statement of his ﷺ is a miracle in that he is informing that it (i.e. Makkah) will remain a Land of Islaam and that the Muslims would have no more need to migrate from it, since most of the fear and insecurity came from its inhabitants. Therefore, the meaning of the hadeeth is: 'There is no more Hijrah after the Conquest (of Makkah) for those who didn't make Hijrah prior to it.' As for making Hijrah from the Lands of Disbelief, then that will remain until the Day of Judgement."

5. Anyone that truly reflects on the saying of the Prophet ﷺ: **"The Muslim is he from whose tongue and hand the Muslims are safe, while the Muhaajir (one who migrates) is he who abandons what Allaah has forbidden"**[97] will comprehend the deeper hidden meaning of what Hijrah contains from good and benefit. A *Muhaajir,* according to the prophetic definition, is one who migrates from and abandons what Allaah has forbidden. So a Muslim should strive hard to abandon things that are unlawful with respect to himself and his state of being, as much as he is able to.

So if someone claims that he has the ability to perform the prayer and pay the Zakaat, as well as establish all of the other rites of Islaam, however he is afflicted by a people that deify and worship cows, while he witnesses this, then this person has not truly abandoned what Allaah has made forbidden. This is since worshipping cows is Shirk, and that is the biggest thing forbidden in the Religion. Likewise, there are those who are tested with having to witness acts of evil and lewd indecency, so their remaining in that land will not enable them to truly abandon what Allaah has made forbidden. This also applies to all of the other things Allaah has made forbidden, which the Muslims are being tested and afflicted with.

Lastly...

Imaam As-Sana'aanee mentioned that the majority of the scholars refuted those who claimed that the hadeeth **"There is no (more) Hijrah after the Conquest"** is general and abrogates all of the *ahaadeeth* about making Hijrah. After quoting the hadeeth: **"I am free from every Muslim that**

[97] Reported by Al-Bukhaaree in his *Saheeh* (no. 10) and Muslim in his *Saheeh* (no. 40)

resides amongst the polytheists", Imaam As-San'aanee said in *Subul-us-Salaam* (4/79):

"The hadeeth is a proof that making Hijrah from (all of) the lands of the polytheists, apart from Makkah, is obligatory. This is the view of the majority of the scholars, which is based on the hadeeth of Jareer ﷺ as well as what has been reported by An-Nasaa'ee from the path of Bahz bin Hakeem who narrated from his father from his grandfather in *marfoo'* form that the Prophet ﷺ said: **'Allaah will not accept a deed from a polytheist after he has accepted Islaam, until he separates from the polytheists.'** It is also based on Allaah's saying:

إِنَّ الَّذِينَ تَوَفَّاهُمُ الْمَلآئِكَةُ ظَالِمِي أَنْفُسِهِمْ قَالُوا فِيمَ كُنتُمْ قَالُوا كُنَّا مُسْتَضْعَفِينَ فِي الأَرْضِ قَالْوَا أَلَمْ تَكُنْ أَرْضُ اللهِ وَاسِعَةً فَتُهَاجِرُوا فِيهَا فَأُوْلَـئِكَ مَأْوَاهُمْ جَهَنَّمُ وَسَاءتْ مَصِيراً

'Verily, as for those whom the angels take (in death) while they are wronging themselves (by not performing Hijrah), they (angels) will say (to them): 'In what (condition) were you?' They will reply: 'We were weak and oppressed in the earth.' They (angels) will say: 'Was not the earth of Allaah spacious enough for you to migrate therein?' Such men will find their abode in Hell - what an evil destination!' [Surah An-Nisaa: 97]

A minority of the scholars have taken the view that Hijrah is not obligatory, and that the *ahaadeeth* (concerning it) are abrogated. They base this on the following hadeeth: Ibn 'Abbaas ﷺ reported that the Messenger of Allaah ﷺ said: **'There is no (more) Hijrah after the Conquest, but instead Jihaad and (good) intention.'** [Agreed upon] They say: It is general and abrogates the existence of Hijrah indicated by the texts mentioned previously. It is also due to the fact that the Prophet ﷺ didn't command those Arabs that accepted Islaam to migrate to him ﷺ, nor did he forbid them from living in their own lands. Also, whenever he ﷺ would send out a military regiment, he ﷺ would say to their leader:

'And when you encounter your enemy from among the polytheists, call them to three things. Whichever of them they agree to, accept it from them and refrain from (fighting) them. Call them to Islaam; if they agree

with you (i.e. they become Muslim), then accept it from them and refrain from (harming) them. Then call them to move from their lands to the land of the Muhaajireen. And inform them that if they do that, they will have what is for the Muhaajireen, and they must abide by what the Muhaajireen are commanded. But if they refuse to move from their lands, inform them that they will be like the Muslim Bedouins - the same rule of Allaah that applies to the (rest of the) believers also applies to them.' [98]

This hadeeth will be stated in its entirety later. Thus, Hijrah was not made obligatory upon these people. As for the other *ahaadeeth* (that obligate Hijrah), apart from the hadeeth of Ibn 'Abbaas, they are with regard to someone who doesn't feel safe about the state of his Religion. They further stated: 'This is a good way of combining (all) of the *ahaadeeth*.'

Those who hold Hijrah to be obligatory responded by saying that the hadeeth: **'There is no (more) Hijrah'** means that it was cancelled out from Makkah, as indicated in his ﷺ saying: **'...after the Conquest'** since migrating from Makkah had been obligatory prior to that (i.e. the Conquest). Ibn Al-'Arabee said: 'Hijrah means leaving from a Land of War (i.e. Disbelief) to a Land of Islaam. It used to be obligatory at the time of Allaah's Messenger ﷺ, and then remained so after his death for whoever feared for his soul. The type of Hijrah that came immediately to an end was that which was done for the aim of seeking out the Prophet ﷺ wherever he was.'"

In short, the correct opinion regarding this issue is that the obligatory Hijrah from Makkah came to an end while Hijrah in its afore-mentioned detailed manner continued to remain. And as for the hadeeth: **"There is no (more) Hijrah after the Conquest"**, this does not abrogate the other texts that mention Hijrah.

---

[98] The entire hadeeth can be found in *Saheeh Muslim* (1731)

The Land is Valuable, but the Religion and Lives of the Muslims are More Valuable

There is no doubt that the lands of the Muslims are valuable. However, the Religion and lives of those who protect these lands, i.e. those who follow the Religion of Truth, are more valuable. And indeed the lands of the Muslims are great. However, the sanctity of the believer is greater, and it is more honorable and supreme. There is nothing better than what has been stated by 'Abdullah bin 'Umar ﷺ when he looked at the Ka'bah one day and said: **"How great you are and how great is your sanctity, yet the believer has a greater sanctity than you!"** [99]

Which Muslim would be pleased with having his honor defamed; or with having some immoral and indecent act be committed against his daughter or sister; or that she be afflicted with regard to her Religion and manners in exchange for the whole world and not just for the sake of one land or region?!

Does Hijrah entail one to neglect his land?

Implementing a portion in the midst of a corrupt whole may seem ridiculous. However this does not cancel out the fact that we should hold this portion as being corrupt. Thus the importance of the portion as it relates to the whole must be made clear, along with a clarification of the importance of acting upon this whole, also.

An example of this: The view that interest is prohibited is from the clear matters over which there is no difference of opinion.

Some people with love for the Religion may call those individuals that work in banks and other interest-based institutions to forsake these places, so those who argue defend themselves by saying: "If all of the workers were to vacate these institutions, this would nullify the people's benefits and cause an increase in robbery and murder."

---

[99] Reported by At-Tirmidhee and Ibn Hibbaan, and it is a sound (*hasan*) hadeeth as referenced in *Ghaayat-ul-Maraam* (435)

Just as the people say with regard to the issue of Hijrah: "Where will the people go", they say: "Where will we put our money? How will we (financially) protect ourselves? What will you do with the ummah's economy, which will most likely collapse? Furthermore, if the Muslims abandon these institutions, the disbelievers and heretics will replace and fill them."

So I say, seeking Allaah's assistance:

In my opinion, the strategy for solving this is to order the workers to abandon these institutions and leave off everything related to interest, while at the same time establishing valid and lawful banks and institutions that are not based on interest. This is with the understanding of the difficulties that will be encountered with the last part (of the strategy) as it relates to our sorrowful state of being.

However, in spite of the fact that this cannot be achieved, this should not cancel out the talk concerning the obligation of leaving these interest-based institutions.

If we were to carry out this informative and intensive campaign regarding the prohibition of interest, and command the people to not cooperate and work with the sin and evil of interest, by way of books, lectures and tapes, the amount of Muslims that would respond - in my imagination - would be equal to only a few, which can hardly be mentioned. And I don't think that getting other Muslims besides them would take a lot of time.

So our current situation says: "The fear of leaving behind all of these institutions for non-Muslims and the fear of the Islamic economy collapsing does not exist at all."

All of the statements and characteristics mentioned previously that are feared will occur should not cancel out talk about the obligation of leaving these interest-based institutions and clarifying the prohibition of dealing with them, in spite of their various forms and types.

And those who pass with flying colors amidst these conflicting views and contradictory beliefs is only that small, small number of people that abandon working in the field of interest, carrying out Allaah's commands and seeking His contentment.

So therefore, it is not correct at all to condemn those who call for the closing of these interest-based institutions and banks with the claim that one is concerned for the benefit and economy of the ummah.

The same applies to the issue of Hijrah - talking about it may seem ridiculous at first due to the conception that Muslims will leave their lands for the enemies of Allaah!

However if the discussion on Hijrah is coupled with talk about preparing oneself for fighting in the Cause of Allaah, the peculiarity (of its topic) would no longer be there. But even if this cannot be achieved, this should not cause us to cancel discussing the ruling on Hijrah, as we have indicated in the example of the workers leaving the interest-based institutions.

Through this method, gaining awareness of its religious ruling will turn into an issue that is essential (to everyone). It is must be started out at first with a few people, then effort must be made to increase that number, then there must be striving, sacrificing and intense preparation applied so that it can become a main concern of the Muslim Khaleefah whom Allaah has designated for solutions to occur at his hands. These are the gradual steps that must be taken. As for terminating all talk concerning it due to the claim that the current affairs are too severe, then this is not correct, since we are required to put the current affairs under the Religion not the Religion under current affairs.

Has the response of those Muslims that live today under the yoke of the disbelievers reached the point that when they heard the verdict on Hijrah they packed their things and flew away from those places in groups and individually?

This is something very far from the reality, unfortunately. So behold there are the orators speaking about the prohibition of interest, yet are its institutes being closed down?!

And they speak about the prohibition and dangers of intermingling between the sexes, yet is it being suppressed and eradicated?!

They speak against singing and musical instruments, yet are they being reduced?!

They talk about the prohibition of backbiting and gossiping, but yet do the people respond?

Yes, there is a response for everything I mentioned above, but it is small and meager.

If the order were to be conveyed to the ummah to undertake this measure and all of them were to do what they felt is pleasing to Allaah, making sacrifices in every manner, the conditions would change and the affairs would be different. This is since this (type of) response is the only path that leads to victory, honor, glory and might.

These are truly signs of change in one's self, which will bring about victory as Allaah, Mighty and Sublime, says:

إِنَّ اللَّهَ لاَ يُغَيِّرُ مَا بِقَوْمٍ حَتَّى يُغَيِّرُوا مَا بِأَنْفُسِهِمْ

"Verily, Allaah will not change the condition of a people until they (first) change what is within themselves." [Surah Ar-Ra'ad: 11]

As for how we can succeed in changing our situation and condition, then at times we may perceive some situations of it and at other times we may not. However, it is our faith and trust in Allaah that enables us to feel at peace. We are certain that Allaah will not break His promise, and that the One who provides us with food from places we don't expect through lawful means is the same One who will provide us with victory from places we don't expect, through valid efforts (on our part), honest faith and correct actions.

Verily, by Allaah, it is Strangeness

By Allaah, it has become necessary for the hearts to grieve and for the eyes to flow with tears after having read what we did from the scholars and Imaams of this ummah, concerning the issue of Hijrah and separating from the polytheists.

It is through their statements that we come to realize how our speakers, teachers, lecturers, writers, authors and critics have improvised and quickly blurted out their opinions and verdicts on this matter, without pondering on the Book of our Lord, Mighty and Sublime, while relying on the *tafseer* of our scholars, without going back to the Sunnah of the Prophet ﷺ, while using the explanations and interpretations of our scholars, and without referring to the statements of the Imaams of our past.

Verily, by Allaah, it is strangeness that we live in during these times.

Authentic knowledge is strange. Correct understanding is strange. Manners of researching are strange. Thorough examination is strange. And the truth is strange.

Indeed the truth is extremely painful and the distress is greatly severe - not just because of what is related to this verdict - even though it has reached the level of seriousness that it has - but rather because this is the methodology that is being followed by many people, especially those who hold role-model and leading positions in most matters and the ability to rule on affairs.

Enthusiasm and sincerity are not sufficient unless they are coupled with knowledge and action.

So let there be a reminder and an admonition for us in this matter.

إِنَّ فِي ذَٰلِكَ لَذِكْرَىٰ لِمَن كَانَ لَهُ قَلْبٌ أَوْ أَلْقَى السَّمْعَ وَهُوَ شَهِيدٌ

"Verily, therein is indeed a reminder for he who has a heart or lends his ear, whilst being heedful." [Surah Qaaf: 37]

O Allaah, make me from those who are sincere, who work hard towards good, and who are strangers, with every honest person that does good deeds while desiring Your Face. And assist us, O Allaah, in this strangeness and its anxieties. Verily, You are Able to do all things.

What has been Said Concerning the one who Praises the Condition of the Jews and Christians

The great scholar Abut-Tayyib Sideeq bin Hasan Al-Bukhaaree said in his book *al-'Ibrah* (pg. 245): "As for the one who praises the Christians and says that they are people of justice or that they love justice, and he constantly commends them at gatherings while speaking lowly about the Muslim leaders, and characterizes the disbelievers with fairness, while removing the attributes of oppression and injustice from them, then the ruling concerning such a person is that he is a disobedient evil-doer that has committed a major sin. It is obligatory upon him to repent and feel remorse for that, if his praise was intended for the nature of the disbelievers, and not the characteristic of disbelief that exists within them.

But if he praises them from the perspective of their disbelief (i.e. that is found within them), then he is a disbeliever. This is since he has in essence praised disbelief, which all of the different forms of Legislation (revealed by Allaah) have condemned.

The Messenger of Allaah ﷺ warned us about praising a Muslim for something about which one has no knowledge, since once when he heard a group of people praising an individual, he ﷺ said: **"You have broken the man's neck"**,[100] meaning you have ruined him.

As for praising the justice found in him in order to endorse him in front of a ruler or to clarify his condition, then this is permissible, rather it is obligatory.

In summary, praising disbelievers due to the disbelief found in them is apostasy in the Religion of Islaam, whereas praising them without having this intention is a major sin. Anyone doing this should be rebuked with that which will prevent him from falling into it.

As for his saying: 'They are people of justice', then if he means by this that the affairs of disbelief, which includes their man-made laws are just, then this is clear and open disbelief. This is since Allaah has condemned and reviled these things, and labeled them with such terms as arrogance,

---

[100] Reported by Al-Bukhaaree (no. 2662) and Muslim (no. 3000)

stubbornness, transgression, a manifest lie, clear sin, supreme loss and slander.

True justice is only that of Allaah's Legislation, which can be found in His Noble Book and the Sunnah of His kind and merciful Prophet ﷺ. Allaah, the Most High, says:

إِنَّ اللَّهَ يَأْمُرُ بِالْعَدْلِ وَالإِحْسَانِ

"Verily, Allaah commands towards justice and goodness..." [Surah An-Nahl: 90]

So if the laws of the Christians were just, we would have been commanded to follow them instead. And this would cause inconsistencies and divergences when refuting them. Allaah says:

أَفَحُكْمَ الْجَاهِلِيَّةِ يَبْغُونَ وَمَنْ أَحْسَنُ مِنَ اللَّهِ حُكْمًا لِّقَوْمٍ يُوقِنُونَ

"Is it the judgement of the Days of Ignorance that they seek after? And who is better in judgement than Allaah for a people that believe with firm Faith." [Surah Al-Maa'idah: 50]

So therefore Allaah's laws are the ones that are the best, not anything else. So how can there be goodness in the laws of the Christians since every form of justice is good while every form of injustice is vile? That which is good is only what the Divine Legislation deems as such, and that which is vile is only what the Divine Legislation deems as such, not the intellect.

Allaah says:

يُرِيدُونَ أَن يَتَحَاكَمُوا إِلَى الطَّاغُوتِ وَقَدْ أُمِرُوا أَن يَكْفُرُوا بِهِ

"They wish to go for judgement (in their disputes) to the *Taaghoot* (false gods and legislations), when they have been ordered to reject them." [Surah An-Nisaa: 60]

These people called what Allaah ordered them to disbelieve in justice, thus going to extremes in their misguidance. And the Devil desires to lead them far astray.

However, if they intended the figurative form of justice, which means building the world, by abandoning injustice, which means the demolishing of the world, then this does not mean that they committed disbelief. However, they should be strongly prevented from doing that."

He said in (pg. 248) of the same book:
"...So whoever belittles the (Muslim) leader while raising the status of disbelief and the leaders of transgression, Allaah will debase him. And whoever is debased by Allaah, no one can bring him honor. So if he belittles the leader with regard to his Islaam while praising the Christians and Jews because of their disbelief, then he has become an apostate.

And if he praises them from the perspective of their building and organizing the world and their protection of their citizens from the different forms of oppression, and because of their spending of wealth in the cause of establishing world order, ascribing the Christians with taking charge of these matters and the (Muslim) ruler with falling short of that, then this person is one who has become overwhelmed with love of this world over love for the Hereafter.

Love for temporary vanities has engrossed his heart, and his goal has removed itself from taking the outer aspects of Islaam into consideration. So he is deceived by the worldly life, and he loves and prefers this present life over the next life. He is afflicted and blindfolded. May Allaah grant refuge to our Muslim brothers from such a condition! Allaah says:

مَن كَانَ يُرِيدُ حَرْثَ الْآخِرَةِ نَزِدْ لَهُ فِي حَرْثِهِ وَمَن كَانَ يُرِيدُ حَرْثَ الدُّنْيَا نُؤْتِهِ مِنْهَا وَمَا لَهُ فِي الْآخِرَةِ مِن نَّصِيبٍ

'Whoever desires (by his deeds) the reward of the Hereafter, We give him increase in his reward. And whoever desires the reward of this world (by his deeds), We give him thereof (what is decreed for him). And he will have no portion (of it) in the Hereafter.' [Surah Ash-Shooraa: 20]

This beguiled individual doesn't realize, due to his ignorance, stupidity, silliness, idiocy and foolishness, that the preservation of the world, which is achieved through the guardianship of the Christians, will detract many times from his Religion. Rather, it may even lead to the obliteration of (all) religious aspects from him, in its totality, since by intermingling with the afore-mentioned disbelievers, their misguided daily practices and laws become commonplace to him. So he deals with interest, sees alcohol and pork, hears the trinity, grows lax with the prayers due to conformity, sees open fornication, hears obscene language, is pleased with the different forms of tax, approves of their unjust systems, and persists upon this state until he becomes attached to that, neither forsaking it nor disapproving of it at all.

And perhaps with the passage of time, he may believe that these laws are permissible due to his overwhelming ignorance. So he has lost his Religion for the sake of attaining his worldly life." [End of quote]

The following is stated in *ar-Rawdat-un-Nawaawiyyah* under the chapter of "Apostasy": "If a schoolteacher tells his students that the Jews are far better than the Muslims since they judge in favor of the rights of the schoolteachers, he has committed disbelief."

It is stated in *Asnaal-Mutaajir* (of Al-Wanshareeshee): "What you mentioned about those emigrants - that they made vile statements, reviled the land of Islaam and longed to return back to the land of polytheism and idols, as well as other evil things which do not come out except from wicked people - all of this brings about disgrace to them in this worldly life and the Hereafter, and puts them in the worst of conditions. It is an obligation upon those in the land, whom Allaah has granted ability and ease, to arrest these people and put them under severe punishment and excruciating torture, by means of beatings and prison time, until they no longer transgress Allaah's limits."

It is also stated in the same book: "As for the statement you quoted from one with inferior intellect and religion that he said: 'Is this the place we should migrate to?' - intending scorn and condescension with that comment, and the statement of the other fool: 'If the ruler of Costello comes to these parts, we will travel to him' and other repulsive and disgusting comments, it is not unknown to your esteemed selves what these two statements contain from repugnance in their intended meaning. It is also quite clear what these two individuals that made such statements possess from deficiency. This is since no one makes such a comment or deems such a statement permissible except for one who has fooled himself and lost his senses - and we seek refuge in Allaah from this." [101]

I say: A Muslim must be broad-minded, but he must not hold good thoughts about the Jews and Christians, for they are the ones who have earned Allaah's anger and gone astray. We know that the Jews sought to deceive Allaah, Mighty and Sublime. Do you think they are not able to deceive human beings and that they are not able to deceive those under their rule, authority and control?!

Verily, they are sinful merchants, trading their Religion, lives, wealth and everything else they own in exchange for a fixed price. So whatever it is that they give you, they take it back from you in multiples. So do not look at what they give you, i.e. such as the ability to voice your word or perform a *rak'ah,* if they permit you to do that.

Rather look at what they have taken and stolen from you. And look at the disbelief, polytheism, and sin that have become beloved to you.

No matter what afflictions, worries and remoteness from the Religion that you find in the lands of the Muslims, there is many times more of that with the Jews and Christians. Seeing one or two crucifixes in a city is better than seeing twenty crucifixes.

And remember the saying of the poet: "**Protecting yourself from some evil is better than experiencing some of it.**"

---

[101] This quote was mentioned in its entirety in the chapter on the statements of the scholars on Hijrah.

The Conclusion

Throughout this research, the reader will note the great esteem the scholars have for the religion of Allaah and their fear of the Muslims being afflicted with regard to their Religion at the hands of their enemies.

They held the view that one must make Hijrah from a land that the Jews and Christians have conquered, not for the sake of abandoning the Muslim dominions (for the disbelievers) - since the scholars are the most eager of people in bringing about benefit to the ummah - but rather to safeguard their Religion, reputation, manners, methodology and lives.

They also warned the Muslims from becoming too accustomed with disbelief and its aspects, fearing that the Muslims may be deceived, subjugated or subdued. They saw Hijrah as being the path leading to Jihaad and held that it was the way to honor and glory. Furthermore, our scholars held that Hijrah was obligatory for every Muslim that feared *fitnah* and was unable to perform the obligatory duties to migrate. And they deemed it recommended for anyone who felt safe (i.e. from afflictions) and had the ability to perform the obligatory duties.

The great scholar Al-Wanshareeshee, may Allaah have mercy on him, has spoken in vast detail about the issue of *fitnah* as it pertains to current times and current understanding, as shown previously. So he has concluded that it is not permissible to reside in these lands based on clear proofs and brilliant arguments, due to the state of being of the wives, children and offspring.

This is the last of what Allaah has granted me the ability to write. I hope that Allaah, Most High, will accept it from me and benefit my Muslim brothers through it. Indeed, He is the All-Hearer, the Responder (of supplications).

Husayn bin 'Awdah Al-'Awaayishah

Appendix A: The Statement of Imaam Muhammad bin 'Abdil-Wahhaab [Died 1206H]

In his famous classical treatise *Thalaathat-ul-Usool,* Imaam Muhammad bin 'Abdil-Wahhaab, may Allaah have mercy on him, said:

Hijrah means: Moving from a Land of Shirk to a Land of Islaam. It is obligatory upon this ummah to migrate from a Land of Shirk to a Land of Islaam, and this is everlasting until the (Final) Hour is established.

The proof for this is Allaah's saying:

إِنَّ الَّذِينَ تَوَفَّاهُمُ الْمَلآئِكَةُ ظَالِمِي أَنْفُسِهِمْ قَالُوا فِيمَ كُنتُمْ قَالُوا كُنَّا مُسْتَضْعَفِينَ فِي الأَرْضِ قَالْوَا أَلَمْ تَكُنْ أَرْضُ اللّهِ وَاسِعَةً فَتُهَاجِرُوا فِيهَا فَأُوْلَـئِكَ مَأْوَاهُمْ جَهَنَّمُ وَسَاءتْ مَصِيرًا . إِلاَّ الْمُسْتَضْعَفِينَ مِنَ الرِّجَالِ وَالنِّسَاء وَالْوِلْدَانِ لاَ يَسْتَطِيعُونَ حِيلَةً وَلاَ يَهْتَدُونَ سَبِيلاً . فَأُوْلَـئِكَ عَسَى اللّهُ أَن يَعْفُوَ عَنْهُمْ وَكَانَ اللّهُ عَفُوًّا غَفُورًا

"Verily, as for those whom the angels take (in death) while they are wronging themselves, they (angels) will say (to them): 'In what (condition) were you?' They will reply: 'We were weak and oppressed in the earth.' They (angels) will say: 'Was not the earth of Allaah spacious enough for you to migrate therein?' Such men will find their abode in Hell - what an evil destination! Except the weak ones among men, women and children - who cannot devise a plan, nor are they able to direct their way. These are the ones whom Allaah is (most) likely to forgive, and Allaah is Ever Oft-Pardoning, Most Forgiving." [Surah An-Nisaa: 97-99]

And Allaah's saying:

يَا عِبَادِيَ الَّذِينَ آمَنُوا إِنَّ أَرْضِي وَاسِعَةٌ فَإِيَّايَ فَاعْبُدُونِ

"O My servants who believe (in Me)! Verily, My earth is spacious so to Me alone, perform your worship." [Surah Al-'Ankaboot: 56]

Al-Baghawee, may Allaah have mercy on him, said: "The reason for the revelation of this *ayah* was due to some Muslims who had resided in Makkah and did not migrate (to Madeenah). Allaah called out to them using the title of Eemaan (for them)."

The proof for Hijrah from the Sunnah is his ﷺ saying: **"Hijrah will not cease until repentance ceases. And repentance will not cease (to be accepted) until the sun rises from where it sets (i.e. the west)."**

So when he settled in Madeenah, he ﷺ commanded all of the remaining Laws of Islaam, such as Zakaat, Fasting, Hajj, Adhaan, Jihaad, commanding good and forbidding evil, as well as the other laws of Islaam. He remained doing this for ten years, and then passed away, praises and peace of Allaah be on him, while his Religion remained.

Appendix B: The Statement of Imaam 'Abdur-Rahmaan bin Qaasim An-Najdee [Died 1392H]

In his explanation of *Thalaathat-ul-Usool,* Imaam 'Abdur-Rahmaan bin Qaasim An-Najdee, may Allaah have mercy on him, said:

The author states: "Hijrah means: Moving from a Land of Shirk to a Land of Islaam." This is in order to preserve one's religion. The Muhaajireen (migrants) were called by this name because they left behind their lands and homes where they had grown up, for the sake of Allaah, and instead joined a land in which they had no family or wealth. This was the case when they migrated to Madeenah. Therefore, everyone that separates himself from his homeland is a Muhaajir (migrant). The root of the word "*Muhaajarah*" comes from breaking away, separating oneself and remaining far away from somebody.

The author says: "It is obligatory upon this ummah to migrate from a Land of Shirk to a Land of Islaam." This is affirmed by the Book, the Sunnah and the unanimous consensus of the scholars. The one who abandons Hijrah is threatened with punishment. Several scholars have relayed that there is consensus on the obligation of Hijrah from a Land of Shirk to a Land of Islaam. In fact, Allaah obligated Hijrah upon His Messenger ﷺ and his Companions before He obligated Fasting and Hajj, as is agreed upon in the books of principles and subsidiary issues, and well known from the Religion by necessity.

His statement: "And this is everlasting until the (Final) Hour is established" is based on the unanimous agreement of the trustworthy scholars. Shaikh-ul-Islaam (Ibn Taimiyyah) said: "One cannot be safe from Shirk unless he remains far away from its adherents."

The author continues: "The proof for this is Allaah's saying: "**Verily, as for those whom the angels take (in death) while they are wronging themselves...**" i.e. by residing amidst the disbelievers. This *ayah* was revealed concerning a group of people from the inhabitants of Makkah who professed Islaam but yet did not migrate. So Allaah says: "**Verily, as for those whom the angels take (in death).**" He is either referring to the Angel of Death and his supporters or just the Angel of Death alone, since the Arabs would speak to one person using the plural form. "**...while they are**

wronging themselves..." by abandoning Hijrah. **"They (angels) will say (to them): 'In what (condition) were you?'"** Meaning: Why did you keep living here and not make Hijrah? This is a rebuking, reprimanding, and scolding type of question. Its meaning is: Why did you continue to live here and not make Hijrah? Which side were you on? This is even though the angels know well what side those who didn't make Hijrah, after it was obligated on them, were on.

Allaah's saying: "**We were weak and oppressed in the earth'** means: "We were not able to make Hijrah. We did not have the ability to leave our land nor to travel through the earth."

"They (angels) will say: 'Was not the earth of Allaah spacious enough for you to migrate therein?'" This refers to Madeenah - such that they migrate to it and abandon the people of Shirk. The angels did not accept their excuse. And in a hadeeth, it states: **"Whoever has intimate ties with a polytheist and resides with him, then he is indeed like him."** [Reported by Abu Dawood and others in various *ahaadeeth*]

Concerning Allaah's statement: **"...Such men will find their abode in Hell - what an evil destination"**, this means: What an evil path to Hell. This shows that the one who abandons Hijrah after it has been made obligatory on him is committing one of the major sins.

Allaah's saying: "...**Except the weak ones among men, women and children..."** refers to those who are unable to make Hijrah. The word "children" here refers to both male and females below the age of puberty.

"Who cannot devise a plan" means: To separate themselves from the polytheists. So these types of people cannot devise a plan or do not have monetary means or power to leave. **"Nor are they able to direct their way"** means: They are not aware of a path leading out from Makkah to Madeenah.

"These are the ones whom Allaah is (most) likely to forgive" meaning: He will pardon those who failed to make Hijrah due to weakness and valid excuses. When Allaah uses "likely" for Himself it is binding since it is something He desires.

"And Allaah is Ever Oft-Pardoning, Most Forgiving." This means that He is Oft-Pardoning, overlooking their trespasses, and Most Forgiving to those who turn to Him in repentance. He does not burden a soul with a responsibility except that He gave it the ability to handle it.

Ibn 'Abbaas said: "My mother and I used to be from among the weak ones, and the Prophet ﷺ would supplicate for the weak ones while in prayer."

Allaah says: **"O My servants who believe (in Me)! Verily, My earth is spacious."** [Surah Al-'Ankaboot: 56] Allaah orders His believing servants to migrate from the land in which they are not able to establish the Religion to His vast earth. So He informs us that the earth is not constricted, but rather vast, encompassing all of the creatures. If a person is in a land in which he cannot openly practice his Religion, then indeed Allaah has made the earth vast for him so that he could worship him in it as He has commanded him.

Hijrah is likewise obligatory upon everyone that resides in a land in which sins are openly committed, and he is not able to change that. Allaah then says: **"So to Me alone, perform your worship."** This means: "Single Me out in worship in My vast earth, which I created as well as everything upon it for you. And I created you upon it to worship Me."

In a *qudsee* hadeeth, Allaah says: **"Son of Aadam, I created you for My sake (i.e. to worship Me.), and I created all things for your sake."**

The author states: "Al-Baghawee, may Allaah have mercy on him, said..." His nickname was Muhyee-us-Sunnah, Abu Muhammad Al-Husayn bin Mas'ood Al-Faraa'. He was the author of the *Tafseer, Sharh-us-Sunnah* and other books. He passed away in 516H.

He (i.e. Al-Baghawee) said: 'The reason for the revelation of this *ayah* was due to some Muslims who had resided in Makkah and did not migrate (to Madeenah). Allaah called out to them using the title of Eemaan (for them)." He reported this on a group amongst the Taabi'een. So he is implying that the one who abandons Hijrah after it has been made obligatory on him is not a disbeliever. Rather, he is sinful and disobedient by having abandoned it. So he is still a believer, but yet has deficient Eemaan. Therefore, he is one of the sinful believers.

The author (i.e. Muhammad bin 'Abdil-Wahhaab) continues: "The proof for Hijrah from the Sunnah is…", i.e. the proof for the obligation of performing Hijrah, from a Land of Shirk to a Land of Islaam, from the Sunnah of Muhammad ﷺ, which we were ordered to follow.

The Prophet ﷺ said: **"Hijrah will not cease until repentance ceases…"** This means: Migrating from a Land of Shirk to a Land of Islaam will not come to an end until repentance comes to an end, i.e. until repentance ceases to be accepted from those who repent. This hadeeth shows that so long as repentance is accepted, Hijrah is obligatory due to its presence.

As for the hadeeth of Ibn 'Abbaas: **"There is no (more) Hijrah after the Conquest (of Makkah), but instead Jihaad and (good) intention"** then what this means is: "There is no (more) Hijrah after the Conquest of Makkah from Makkah to Madeenah since Makkah had become a Land of Islaam after it was conquered." This was since a group of people wanted to migrate from Makkah to Madeenah thinking that this was something encouraged. So the Prophet ﷺ explained to them that he only encouraged this when Makkah was a Land of Disbelief.

But as for when it had become a Land of Islaam, then it did not apply anymore. Therefore, the hadeeth means: **"There is no (more) Hijrah from Makkah to Madeenah."** But as for the establishment and continuity of Hijrah from the Lands of Shirk to the Lands of Islaam, then this is well-known by way of the texts and unanimous agreement. [102]

---

[102] Refer to *Jaami' Shurooh al-Usool–uth-Thalaathah* (pg. 745-748)

Appendix C: The Statement of Imaam Muhammad Amaan bin 'Alee Al-Jaamee [Died 1406H]

In his explanation of *Thalaathat-ul-Usool*, Imaam Muhammad Amaan Al-Jaamee, may Allaah have mercy on him, said:

The author states: "Hijrah means: Moving from a Land of Shirk to a Land of Islaam." According to its religious definition, Hijrah means: Moving from a Land of Shirk to a Land of Islaam. So if this is the case, then how can we call the migration that the Sahaabah (Companions) made from Makkah to Abyssinia Hijrah?! Abyssinia was not a Land of Islaam, rather it was a Land of Disbelief. Even though disbelief is at different levels, they were still Christians from the People of the Scripture.

The Companions migrated from the abuse of the polytheists. And yet, the country of Abyssinia was not a Land of Islaam. So then, can the term "Hijrah" be applied to that journey and travel that the Companions made to Abyssinia? The answer to this is: Yes, it can be applied to it from a linguistic sense. Linguistically, Hijrah means to move from one place to another. You will always notice that the linguistic meaning of a word is broader and more general than its religious meaning. So the mere act of moving from one land is called Hijrah, according to the language. However, according to the religious meaning, it is not called Hijrah unless it takes place from a Land of Disbelief to a Land of Islaam. So therefore, the "Hijrah" that the Companions made, after careful analysis, is not the Hijrah that is well known, but rather, it was a journey for the sake of Calling and Conveying the Message, and so that they could spread the New Call to the African Continent.

This is what alarmed the people of Makkah to the point that they said: "The Call has left. The Call of the man (i.e. Muhammad) has gone to Africa to Najaashee." He was known to them. So they were worried so much so that they chose and dispatched a delegation led by the cleverest amongst the leading men of the Arabs, 'Amr bin Al-'Aas.[103] They equipped him with all the information he would need and the gifts that were loved by the kings of Abyssinia. So they arrived and came in contact with the king and the members of his palace. And they covered the land with gifts, as it is

[103] **Translator's Note:** This was before he became a Muslim.

commonly said, in order that their request could be accepted. What was their request? It was that they hand over that delegation to them. 'Amr described them as being foolish. This is how the people of falsehood always are - they describe the people of truth as being foolish, crazy and having little understanding - i.e. foolish. They said: "They have abandoned the religion of their forefathers and won't accept your religion (either)."

It was as if he meant to say: There doesn't exist any religion except for our religion and your religion, O Najaashee. And these individuals do not adhere to your religion or the religion of your forefathers. And the proof for this is that when they enter into your presence, they don't prostrate to you with the greeting due to Abyssinian kings since they are irrational.

Upon hearing this about them, he summoned them. And they were standing outside. So they came in with Ja'far bin Abee Taalib leading them. He stopped by the door and raised his voice, saying: "The Party of Allaah seeks your permission to enter" in his loudest voice. This was a strange voice from a strange man. He asked them to repeat, so Ja'far said again: "The Party of Allaah seeks your permission to enter!" An-Najaashee realized that these were no ordinary people, so he said: "Let them enter."

They then entered into his presence, with Ja'far leading them, and their heads raised up and not bending their backs - i.e. standing. At this, An-Najaashee asked: "Why don't you prostrate to me, i.e. greet me like my people greet me?" Ja'far replied: "We only prostrate to the One who put you in charge, not to you."

"We only prostrate to the One who put you in charge" refers to Allaah, the One who made you a king. He gives the rule to whom He wills and takes it away from whom He wills. The One who made you a king is the One that deserves to be worshipped and prostrated to. This moved An-Najaashee, so he began asking them about the new religion and about the new messenger and what he came with and what befell him.

In brief, he acknowledged the truth, gave back the gifts to the delegation from Quraysh, and then expelled them. So they returned home debased and unsuccessful. When An-Najaashee honored these Companions of Allaah's Messenger, which consisted of members from the Prophet's Household, not to mention some of his daughters, Allaah honored him with Islaam. So he became the first king of his time that believed in the Messenger of Allaah ﷺ and openly professed his Faith.

This is what is meant by the Companions' "Hijrah" (migration) to Abyssinia - it was not the well-known and recognized form of Hijrah. Rather, it was a means of calling to Allaah, conveying His Message, and explaining His new Religion so that the people there could be aware of it, and so that the Call could spread and transcend the Arab Peninsula. This is the objective of Hijrah.

The author states: "It is obligatory upon this ummah to migrate from a Land of Shirk to a Land of Islaam, and this is everlasting until the (Final) Hour is established."

Certain forms of Hijrah exist today. Some Muslims migrate after having been harassed and oppressed in their homelands, not being able to openly practice their Religion and feeling tired of being followed and interrogated. So they migrate to some of the European countries and there, they are able to establish the rites of the Religion and build mosques and schools.

It has reached me that in France there is a city that has transformed to the point that it looks like an Arab Islamic city due to the large amount of mosques and schools there. This was established by some of the Arabs that had migrated there. There is no need to mention their country of origin now. These brothers often come to visit us during Hajj, and they call us by telephone and attend the lessons and record them. And they take back with them information from the two sacred sites (*Haramain*) through the means of recording, and then spread the correct Call (Da'wah) over there by way of tapes. So the Call to the Methodology of the Salaf has spread, all praise be to Allaah. These individuals are always in contact with us, visiting us on every special occasion. And they are always inviting the people of knowledge here to observe the fast (i.e. during Ramadaan) with them (in their city) - so some of them do it, if they are able.

And they come in droves during the time of Hajj. They do more for the Da'wah (Call) than we do. There is no comparison between our actions and their actions. We do work while living in an Islamic country, feeling secure about our property and our lives and everything, whereas these individuals do work while in a Land of Disbelief. Through their hard work and efforts, they were able to transform, by Allaah's Grace, cities until they turned into Lands of Islaam. Some of the people of knowledge have issued religious rulings to them, informing them that their city had become a Land of Islaam and that they should live there and not be disturbed, and that they should not say: "We have migrated from a Land of Islaam to a Land of Disbelief" since they were able to change their city to a Land of Islaam. And to Allaah belongs the Praise and Grace.

Certain forms of Hijrah can be found like this during these times. There are many Muslims, including Arabs that are oppressed in their lands, and so they have become strangers. So they make Hijrah and thus Allaah grants them success in those lands where they are able to live with their heads raised high, calling to the Religion of Allaah with freedom.

This is similar to the Hijrah performed by the Companions when they migrated to Abyssinia, where they lived worshipping Allaah freely after having been oppressed in their countries.

But as for individual Muslims migrating to Europe and to America and to countries in the east (Asia) to live individually amongst the disbelievers and not being able to openly practice the tenets of their Faith and perhaps, as we have been informed, being forced to abandon the Dhuhr and 'Asr prayers and to combine their prayers from night to day to the point that they deliberately leave off the Jumu'ah (Friday) Prayer, since the day off for them is Sunday and not Friday, for that's a work day...'Abdur-Rahmaan is forced to obey George, the company manager...George says to him: "Sunday is a day off for us and Friday is not. If you want, you can work with us, and if not, you can leave"....So he lives there with the life of an animal - eating, drinking, cohabitating, etc. - he has nothing more than this, since he has abandoned his Religion...such a lifestyle is not permissible.

Whoever is afflicted with this type of Hijrah - i.e. migrating alone to live amidst the disbelievers in a debased manner, having forgotten the glory of Islaam and the meaning of:

وَلِلَّهِ الْعِزَّةُ وَلِرَسُولِهِ وَلِلْمُؤْمِنِينَ

"To Allaah belongs the glory, and to His Messenger and the Believers"[104] living under the management of George, lowering himself to him, bowing his head before him, saying: "Yes, sir", asking for a day off and George does not grant it, then such a lifestyle is *Haraam* (unlawful).

It is not lawful for a Muslim to live his life in such a manner while in a land that is not a Land of Islaam. If a Muslim is harmed in his country and there is a Muslim country that he is able to live in and worship Allaah freely, feeling secure about his life, property and Religion, he is obligated to make Hijrah to this (Muslim) land.

This is unless his remaining in his country, in spite of the harm he endures in it, has a beneficial advantage for the Call to Islaam. His life and property may be subject to danger, however his remaining there has a (positive) effect. An example of this is if he is a student of knowledge or one of the scholars, and he is able to spread knowledge and the Call secretly in his home or in any occasion he gets, whilst being patient with the oppression.

A person such as this should not make Hijrah. Rather, he should remain there and be patient with the harm. This is so long as he is not ordered to commit open disbelief and so long as he is not restricted from praying. But in the case where he just faces harm to his life and his property (and not his Religion), then he should be patient and spread the Call there.

We have stated that Hijrah linguistically means moving from one place to another, while religiously, it means migrating from a Land of Shirk to a Land of Eemaan or moving from a Land of Insecurity to a Land of Security. This second portion of its religious definition was noted by Imaam An-Nawawee. So according to the second definition, it is correct to apply the term "Hijrah" to the migration that the Companions of Allaah's Messenger ﷺ made to Abyssinia.

And if not, then according to the first definition, their move was not from a Land of Disbelief to a Land of Islaam, but rather it was a move from a Land of Insecurity and Instability and Fear for one's Religion and property to a Land of Security and Safety. They lived in a place in which they feared for their Religion and lives and feared worshipping Allaah. So they moved to a

---

[104] Surah Al-Munaafiqoon: 8

place where they were able to gain security in their Religion, lives and worship.

Based on this understanding, it is correct to apply the term "Hijrah", in the religious sense, to the journey the Companions of Allaah's Messenger ﷺ made to Abyssinia. And if this is not the case, then their Hijrah was in the linguistic sense, and the objective behind it was, as we stated before, to spread the Call and to convey the new Religion and the message of the last of the prophets, Muhammad ﷺ, to the people in Africa.

The author states: "It is obligatory upon this ummah to migrate from a Land of Shirk to a Land of Islaam, and this is everlasting until the (Final) Hour is established." This was such that some of the Imaams, such as Imaam Maalik, said: "If a person is in a land in which the pious predecessors (Salaf as-Saalih) are reviled and he is not able to prevent them, it is obligatory to make Hijrah from that place." This means that if a Muslim is afflicted with living amongst the enemies of the Companions of Allaah's Messenger ﷺ and the Taabi'een, and they revile them out loud and he is not able to oppose them or prevent them, it is not permissible for him to remain there with them. Rather, he is obligated to depart and migrate from that place to another place. Imaam Maalik issued a statement in this regard.

"The proof for this" i.e. for the obligation of Hijrah "is Allaah's saying":

إِنَّ الَّذِينَ تَوَفَّاهُمُ الْمَلآئِكَةُ ظَالِمِي أَنْفُسِهِمْ قَالُوا فِيمَ كُنتُمْ قَالُوا كُنَّا مُسْتَضْعَفِينَ فِي الأَرْضِ

"Verily, as for those whom the angels take (in death) while they are wronging themselves, they (angels) will say (to them): 'In what (condition) were you?' They will reply: 'We were weak and oppressed in the earth.'" [Surah An-Nisaa: 97]

This *ayah,* as stated by Imaam Al-Baghawee and other scholars, was revealed with regard to a group of people that professed Islaam but did not migrate. They professed the statement of Islaam, bearing witness that there is no deity worthy of worship except Allaah and that Muhammad is the Messenger of Allaah ﷺ, but in spite of this, they didn't make Hijrah along with the Messenger of Allaah ﷺ to the Messenger of Allaah ﷺ. Rather they remained with the polytheists in Makkah.

At this time, Hijrah was a condition for the acceptance of Islaam. Whoever embraced Islaam was obligated to join the Messenger of Allaah ﷺ, and it was not permissible for him to remain in Makkah. But these people did not leave Makkah. So when the polytheists set out to fight in the Battle of Badr, these individuals went out with them to fight against the Muslims, and so they ended up getting killed. Therefore, this verse was revealed about them: **"Verily, as for those whom the angels take (in death) while they are wronging themselves."** They are wronging themselves by remaining amongst the polytheists after having professed the statement of Islaam. And they are considered as being from among the polytheists. So the angels will beat their faces and backs, saying to them: **"In what (condition) were you?"** What group were you from? **"In what (condition) were you?"** What were you upon - Islaam or Shirk? This is a question that denotes reprimanding, scolding and condemning.

"They will reply" making excuses for themselves: **"We were weak and oppressed in the earth."** Allaah knew that this excuse was false, so he did not accept excuses from them. **"They (angels) will say: 'Was not the earth of Allaah spacious enough for you to migrate therein?"** What falls under the "Earth of Allaah" first and foremost is the city of Madeenah. The vast earth of Allaah consists of Madeenah - so why didn't you migrate there?

"Such men will find their abode in Hell - what an evil destination!" This is proof that Allaah did not accept their excuse, and that their excuse was invalid and an unacceptable justification. This is why Allaah pardoned those whom He knew had valid excuses, as He says: **"Except the weak ones among men, women and children - who cannot devise a plan, nor are they able to direct their way."**

Allaah excused these types of people - women, children, and incapacitated men - who could not migrate and remained amongst the polytheists. Allaah excused them, saying: **"These are the ones whom Allaah is (most) likely to forgive, and Allaah is Ever Oft-Pardoning, Most Forgiving."**

'Abdullaah bin 'Abbaas ؓ stated that he and his mother were from those excused due to their weakness and inability, and that they were from those whose excuse was accepted by Allaah. In the same manner, if a person is honest with Allaah and Allaah is aware of his excuse and inability and lack of a way of getting out, He will accept his excuse and pardon him. This principle can be applied to all matters. Allaah is not fooled by anything - not even by what some people do today who seek refuge in the name of Islaam, calling out and proclaiming the name of Islaam when things are difficult for them, but in reality, they are callers against Islaam and enemies of Islaam. Allaah is not fooled by these things.

The servant must be honest with Allaah. So whoever is truthful in his excuses, his Islaam, and his adherence to the Religion of Allaah, Allaah will accept his excuse. And whoever is not, Allaah will not accept it.

The first group of people mentioned in the *ayah* gave the excuse: **"We were weak and oppressed in the earth."** Allaah did not accept this excuse because they were not truthful. However, He accepted the excuse of those who were unable to migrate (i.e. the second group of people), saying about them: **"These are the ones whom Allaah is (most) likely to forgive."** When the word *'asaa* (most likely) is stated with respect to Allaah it means that it is binding (i.e. it will definitely happen) and not that it is something hoped for. **"And Allaah is Ever Oft-Pardoning, Most Forgiving."** What we also derive from this is that whenever Allaah obligates or prohibits something, He always makes exceptions to the rule (for certain individuals), due to Wisdom from Himself and Mercy towards His servants.

Allaah obligated Hijrah upon everyone that believed to the point that their excuses and proclamation of Islaam were not accepted until they migrated. This was before the Conquest of Makkah. This Hijrah and obligation came to an end with the Conquest of Makkah, but before this, no one's claim to Islaam was accepted until he had migrated. This was an established principle (at that time). But in spite of that, Allaah exempted those who were weak, those who were forced to stay and those who could not find a way to travel.

When Allaah prohibited the meat of dead animals, blood, and swine, He exempted from this those who were forced due to an emergency to eat dead animals, the meat of swine, and blood, out of Mercy from Himself. You will not find, even if you search and investigate throughout the entire Book of Allaah, a rule such as this except that you will find with it an exemption.

The scholars who derive principles have taken these exemptions and derived a rule from them, which states: **"Cases of Emergency make the Forbidden Permissible."**

Similar to this is the case of the polytheist man who followed the Messenger of Allaah ﷺ on the day of the Battle of Badr and said to him: "O Messenger of Allaah ﷺ, I want to follow you and gain with you what you gain." So he ﷺ said to him: **"Do you believe in Allaah and His Messenger?"** The man said: "No.' So the Messenger of Allaah ﷺ said: **"Go back for I will never seek the assistance of a polytheist."** So he went back, but came to him a second time, saying to him: "I want to follow you to acquire from that which you acquire (i.e. of war booty)." The Prophet ﷺ said to him: **"Do you believe in Allaah and His Messenger?"** The man said: "No." So the Messenger of Allaah ﷺ said: **"Go back for I will never seek the assistance of a polytheist."** Then he came to him a third time, saying to him the same thing he said in his first and second encounters with him. So the Messenger of Allaah ﷺ asked him again: **"Do you believe in Allaah and His Messenger?"** The man said: "Yes." So the Prophet ﷺ said: **"Go."** And so he fought alongside him.

The people of knowledge differ on the guidelines found in this hadeeth. Some of them say that the Messenger of Allaah ﷺ only did this because he knew that this man would eventually become Muslim – i.e. if he turned him back once or twice, he would eventually embrace Islaam. He knew this through revelation. This is why he turned him back the first and second time until Allaah blessed him with Islaam and so he followed the Messenger of Allaah and fought alongside him. The scholars who hold this view are Imaam Abu Haneefah and the scholars that follow his *madh'hab*.

Many scholars believe that it is permissible to receive the assistance of a polytheist over another polytheist. So therefore the objective behind this hadeeth was not to institute a prohibition, but rather, its objective was to incite a person towards Islaam. The proof for this is that the Messenger of Allaah ﷺ sought the assistance of Safwaan bin Umayyah in the Battle of Hunain, and he was a polytheist. And he allowed a man, whom he knew through revelation that he was a disbeliever and from the inhabitants of the Hellfire, to fight in one of the battles – I believe it was the Battle of Uhud. He would fight strongly and kill many people to the point that the Companions were amazed by him.

But the Prophet ﷺ would say that he was from the inhabitants of Hell. The Companions were baffled by this news. Here was a man that endured a good trial such as this in front of the Messenger of Allaah ﷺ and yet the Messenger of Allaah ﷺ says about him that he is from the inhabitants of Hell?? So one of the Companions followed him to find out what his fate would be. In the end, the man was wounded badly while fighting and could not endure the pain, so he fell upon his sword and killed himself. The Messenger of Allaah ﷺ was informed of what took place, so he said: **"Bear witness that I am the Messenger of Allaah ﷺ."** Then he ﷺ said: **"Verily, Allaah will surely aid this Religion through an evil man."** But in spite of this (i.e. that he was destined for Hell), the Messenger of Allaah ﷺ did not prevent him from participating in the battle.

Those who hold this view believe that it is permissible to receive assistance from a disbeliever over another disbeliever. As for those who hold the other view, they take the apparent understanding of the hadeeth reported by Imaam Muslim from 'Aa'ishah ؓ concerning the story of the man who came to the Messenger ﷺ twice. Whoever takes this hadeeth in its literal apparent sense without investigating into its detailed understanding, says: "It is not permissible to seek the assistance of a disbeliever unless in cases of necessity." Imaam Ash-Shaafi'ee has been quoted as stating that it is disliked to receive assistance from them except in cases of necessity.

Moreover, are you able to distinguish between a case of necessity and a case of an emergency? What is the difference between a necessity and an emergency? There is a huge difference between the two. Some scholars considered it disliked to receive assistance from polytheists if there was no case of necessity. But as for cases of emergency, receiving assistance from them is either permissible or obligatory, just as in the examples of eating the meat of dead carcasses. Eating the meat of a dead carcass can either be permissible or obligatory. If you have a valid necessity for eating the meat of a carcass, it is permissible to eat one. But if you are compelled to do so, i.e. out of an emergency, then it becomes obligatory.

So the difference between a necessity and an emergency is: If you are thirsty and want to drink water, which if you don't drink, no harm will befall you – this is called a necessity. But in the case where you urgently require drinking water to the point that if you don't drink it, destructive harm will befall you, you become obligated to drink. This is the same case with eating the meat of a dead carcass and with the issue of receiving assistance from the disbelievers. Likewise, if there exists a case of an emergency such that you fear for your life, your Religion, your sacred things, your country, and your nation if you don't get assistance, after Allaah's aid from the disbelievers and you request their aid in this type of emergency situation, then receiving assistance from them becomes obligatory whereas in cases of non-emergency, such as a normal necessity, receiving assistance from them is permissible.

This is the view of those scholars who hold that it is not permissible at all to receive aid from the disbelievers. As for those who hold the first view, they believe that it is allowed to receive their aid in the absolute sense, and they explain that the Prophet ﷺ only prevented that polytheist man from following him because of what we mentioned previously that he ﷺ knew he would become a Muslim.

Al-Haafidh Ibn Hajr held another view, which was that receiving aid from the disbelievers was not allowed based on that hadeeth, however it was allowed based on the story of Safwaan. In any case, the Fiqh principle that the students of knowledge should understand is: **"When Allaah forbids something and stresses its forbiddance, we find that He makes exceptions in cases of emergency."** Amongst these cases of emergency is that which we are discussing now.

Among the proofs for the obligation of Hijrah is Allaah's saying:

يَا عِبَادِيَ الَّذِينَ آمَنُوا إِنَّ أَرْضِي وَاسِعَةٌ فَإِيَّايَ فَاعْبُدُونِ

"O My servants who believe (in Me)! Verily, My earth is spacious so to Me alone, perform your worship." [Surah Al-'Ankaboot: 56] You are not compelled to remain under duress and persecution. Leave from the Land of Disbelief to a Land of Islaam and worship Allaah there, or from the Land of Fear and Instability to a Land of Security and Stability and worship Allaah there.

Hijrah was obligatory, based on these verses, up until Makkah was conquered. However, the (general) obligation of Hijrah from a place of

Shirk, persecution and revilement against the Muslims and Islaam to a place in which this is not heard of continued to remain obligatory.

Al-Baghawee, may Allaah have mercy on him, said: 'The reason for the revelation of this *ayah* was due to some Muslims who had resided in Makkah and did not migrate (to Madeenah). Allaah called out to them using the title of Eemaan (for them)."

The author is referring to the last *ayah* mentioned from Surah Al-'Ankaboot. The author states: "The proof for Hijrah from the Sunnah is his ﷺ saying: **'Hijrah will not cease until repentance ceases. And repentance will not cease (to be accepted) until the sun rises from where it sets (i.e. the west).'**

The Hijrah that "will not cease" here does not refer to the Hijrah that was obligatory from Makkah to Madeenah since this type of Hijrah ended with the Conquest of Makkah. Rather, what is being referred to here is the Hijrah from the Land of Shirk to the Land of Islaam, as has been clarified in the explanation. [105]

---

[105] Refer to *Jaami' Shurooh al-Usool–uth-Thalaathah* (pg. 748-757), which is a large book containing a compilation of explanations from several scholars of Imaam Muhammad bin 'Abdil-Wahhaab's famous treatise *Thalaathat-ul-Usool.*

Appendix D: The Statement of Imaam Muhammad Naasir-ud-Deen Al-Albaanee [Died 1420H]

Commenting on the prophetic hadeeth: **"Verily, if you testify that there is no deity that has the right to be worshipped except Allaah, and you establish the prayer and give the Zakaat and disassociate from the polytheists, and you give a fifth from the spoils of war, as well as the Prophet's share and what he is allowed to pick from it before its distribution, then you will be protected with the security of Allaah and the security of His Messenger"**, Imaam Al-Albaanee said:

There are some rulings in this hadeeth that are related to calling the disbelievers to Islaam. From these rulings is that they will have security if they establish what Allaah has obligated upon them. Also from among them is dissociating from the polytheists and migrating to the lands of the Muslims. There are many *ahaadeeth* reported about this, all of which revolve around encouraging the one who accepts Islaam to abandon the disbelievers. An example of this is his ﷺ statement: **"I am free from every Muslim that resides amongst the polytheists...Their fires should not be visible to one another."**

In other narrations, the Prophet ﷺ made it a condition when pledging allegiance to him that one must disassociate himself from the polytheists. In other narrations, he ﷺ said: **"Allaah does not accept a deed from a polytheist after he accepts Islaam until he leaves from the polytheists to (go to) the Muslims."**

And there are many other *ahaadeeth*, some of which I have referenced in *Irwaa-ul-Ghaleel* (5/29-33) and some which have preceded under number: 636. [106]

From the things that are extremely unfortunate is that those who accept Islaam in current times - in spite of their large number, all praise be to Allaah - do not respond to this ruling of disassociating from the disbelievers and migrating to the Lands of Islaam, except for a few amongst them. I attribute this to two reasons:

---

[106] **Translator's Note:** He is referring here to his monumental compilation *Silsilat-ul-Ahaadeeth as-Saheehah* from where this quote was taken.

First: Their greediness for the worldly luxuries, easy means of living and extravagant lifestyle found in their countries on the basis that they are already living a pleasant materialistic life with no spirit in it, as is well known. Therefore, it is difficult for them to move to a Muslim country in which the means of good living are not as abundant for them, according to their perception.

Second: The other, and this is the most important, is their ignorance of this ruling. If this is the case, they are excused, since they did not hear about it from any of the callers whose words are widespread and translated into several foreign languages, or from those who go to them in the name of Da'wah. This is since most of them are not Fuqahaa (Jurisprudent scholars). This is especially the case with those among them from the Jamaa'at at-Tableegh, for instead these people only increase their attachment to their countries because of the fact that they see that many Muslims have reversed this ruling by abandoning their own countries to go to the countries of the disbelievers! So how can these individuals whom Allaah has guided to Islaam come to be aware of the likes of this ruling when the Muslims themselves are contradicting it?!

These individuals as well as those (Muslims that leave the Muslim lands) should know for certainty that Hijrah is permanent and ongoing just like Jihaad, as the Prophet ﷺ said: **"Hijrah will not come to an end so long as the enemy continues to be fought."** And in another hadeeth, he ﷺ said: **"Hijrah will not cease until repentance ceases. And repentance will not cease (to be accepted) until the sun rises from where it sets."** This hadeeth is referenced in *Irwaa-ul-Ghaleel* (1208).

From that which must be known is that Hijrah is of various types and that it has numerous causes, which requires a separate occasion to explain. What's important here is that migrating from the Lands of Disbelief to the Lands of Islaam - regardless of whether the rulers of those lands (of Islaam) have deviated from Islaam or just fallen short in applying its laws - is good compared to the indescribable manners, religious qualities and behavior found in the Lands of Disbelief. The matter is not like that which has been claimed by one of the foolish and hasty ignorant speakers, when he said:

"By Allaah, if I had a choice between living in Jerusalem under Jewish occupation and living in any Arab capital, I would definitely choose to live in Jerusalem under Jewish occupation!"

He added to this saying: "I do not hold except that Hijrah is obligatory from Algeria to Tel Aviv!!"

This is what he said, may his mouth be severed! And the falsehood of such a statement is not hidden to the Muslim - not even the simple-minded one among them!

In order to bring home, what I mentioned previously from goodness, to the minds of the readers who love the truth and strive to learn and follow it - those who are not frightened by the cries of the criers, the screams of the performers or the instability of the instigators from among the jealous and malicious speakers and writers - I say to these loved ones:

Remember, at the least, two hadeeths from the Messenger of Allaah ﷺ:

First: **"Verily, Eemaan (Faith) returns to Madeenah just as the snake returns to its burrow."**

Reported by Al-Bukhaaree, Muslim and others.

Second: **"There will not cease to be a group from my ummah triumphant upon the truth, until the Command of Allaah comes while they are still triumphant."**

This is an authentic *mutawaatir* hadeeth that has been reported by a group amongst the Companions. I previously mentioned the references from a number of them under no. 270, 1108, 1955 and 1956, and in *Saheeh Abee Dawood* (no. 1245). In some narrations, it states that they are the "Inhabitants of Maghrib", i.e. Shaam. The explanation of this has been reported in Al-Bukhaaree and others from Mu'aadh ؓ and in At-Tirmidhee. Others raised it to a saying of the Prophet ﷺ with the wording:

"If the inhabitants of Shaam become corrupt, then there is no good in you. And there will not cease to be a group from my ummah..."

There is a strong indication in these *ahaadeeth* that with regard to lands, consideration is given to its inhabitants and not its borders. Salmaan Al-Faarisee ﷺ clarified this fact when Abud-Dardaa ﷺ wrote to him requesting him to come to the holy lands (in Jerusalem). So Salmaan wrote back to him, saying: **"Indeed, the holy lands do not sanctify anyone. Rather it is only a person's deeds that sanctify him."** [*Al-Muwatta'* of Imaam Maalik (2/235)]

Therefore it is from tremendous ignorance and profound stupidity - if not to say from little religion - that this stupid speaker would choose to reside under Jewish occupation and mandate upon the persecuted Algerians that they should have to migrate to Tel Aviv and not his own Muslim city, 'Amman, for example, rather not even to Makkah and Madeenah, pretending to be unaware of the evil, immorality and depravity the Jews are spreading in Palestine generally and in Tel Aviv, Haifa and Yafa in particular. This is such that these acts have spread onto many of the Muslim men and women by virtue of their living in the vicinity and being contaminated by it. This is quite clear to those who lived with them and then were saved by Allaah or those who regularly go back to visit their families there on occasion.

It is quite apparent to everyone that has been given some knowledge that there is a clear contradiction between this "choice" made by the speaker and Allaah's statement:

إِنَّ الَّذِينَ تَوَفَّاهُمُ الْمَلآئِكَةُ ظَالِمِي أَنْفُسِهِمْ قَالُوا فِيمَ كُنتُمْ قَالُوا كُنَّا مُسْتَضْعَفِينَ فِي الأَرْضِ قَالْوَا أَلَمْ تَكُنْ أَرْضُ اللّهِ وَاسِعَةً فَتُهَاجِرُوا فِيهَا فَأُوْلَـئِكَ مَأْوَاهُمْ جَهَنَّمُ وَسَاءتْ مَصِيرًا . إِلاَّ الْمُسْتَضْعَفِينَ مِنَ الرِّجَالِ وَالنِّسَاء وَالْوِلْدَانِ لاَ يَسْتَطِيعُونَ حِيلَةً وَلاَ يَهْتَدُونَ سَبِيلاً . فَأُوْلَـئِكَ عَسَى اللّهُ أَن يَعْفُوَ عَنْهُمْ وَكَانَ اللّهُ عَفُوًّا غَفُورًا . وَمَن يُهَاجِرْ فِي سَبِيلِ اللّهِ يَجِدْ فِي الأَرْضِ مُرَاغَمًا كَثِيراً وَسَعَةً وَمَن يَخْرُجْ مِن بَيْتِهِ مُهَاجِرًا إِلَى اللّهِ وَرَسُولِهِ ثُمَّ يُدْرِكْهُ الْمَوْتُ فَقَدْ وَقَعَ أَجْرُهُ عَلى اللّهِ وَكَانَ اللّهُ غَفُورًا رَّحِيمًا

"Verily, as for those whom the angels take (in death) while they are wronging themselves (by not performing Hijrah), they (angels) will say

(to them): 'In what (condition) were you?' They will reply: 'We were weak and oppressed in the earth.' They (angels) will say: 'Was not the earth of Allaah spacious enough for you to migrate therein?' Such men will find their abode in Hell - what an evil destination! Except the weak ones among men, women and children - who cannot devise a plan, nor are they able to direct their way. These are the ones whom Allaah is (most) likely to forgive, and Allaah is Ever Oft-Pardoning, Most Forgiving. And whoever migrates in the Way of Allaah, he will find many dwelling places and plenty (of sustenance) to live by. And whoever leaves his home as an emigrant unto Allaah and His Messenger, and death overtakes him, his reward is then surely incumbent upon Allaah, and Allaah is Ever Oft-Forgiving, Most Merciful." [Surah An-Nisaa: 97-100]

Al-Haafidh Ibn Katheer said in his *Tafseer* (1/542): "Thus this noble *ayah* was revealed, generally applying to everyone that resides amongst the disbelievers, (1) whilst possessing the ability to make Hijrah and (2) not being able to establish his Religion in that land. So (in this case) he is oppressing himself and committing the forbidden. This is based on the consensus of the scholars, and also on the wording found in this *ayah*."

And verily, that in which the Muslim scholar has no doubt about is that this verse, in the general sense, indicates more than just Hijrah from the lands of the disbelievers. Imaam Al-Qurtubee clearly stated this in his *Tafseer* (5/346) when he said: "There is proof in this *ayah* for migrating from the land in which acts of disobedience are practiced. Sa'eed bin Jubair said: 'If sins are practiced in a land, then leave from it.' And he recited the verse: **'Was not the earth of Allaah spacious enough for you to migrate therein?'"**

This narration was reported by Ibn Abee Haatim in his *Tafseer* (2/174/1) with an authentic chain of narration from Sa'eed. Al-Haafidh (Ibn Hajr) indicated it in *Fat'h-ul-Baaree* (8/263), saying: "Sa'eed bin Jubair derived from this verse that Hijrah is obligatory from a land in which acts of disobedience are (openly) practiced."

Some ignorant people from amongst the speakers, Doctorate holders and professors think that the Prophet's statement: **"There is no (more) Hijrah**

after the Conquest"[107] abrogates Hijrah in the absolute sense. This is disgraceful ignorance of the Book and the Sunnah and the statements of the Imaams. I have heard such remarks coming from one of the professors who claims to have knowledge during a debate that occurred between him and I due to the calamity which that speaker I mentioned before brought down upon me. But when I reminded him of the previously mentioned hadeeth that clearly states Hijrah will not come to an end, with the wording: **"Hijrah will not cease..."**, he was not able to respond! [108]

At this point, I would like to quote for the noble readers what Shaikh-ul-Islaam Ibn Taimiyyah said about the two afore-mentioned hadeeths, stating that there is no contradiction between them. He said in *Majmoo'-ul-Fataawaa* (18/281):

"Both of them are true. The first one refers to the Hijrah that was specific for its time frame, and that was the Hijrah from Makkah and other Arab lands to Madeenah. This is since this Hijrah was legislated at the time that Makkah and these other lands were still Lands of Disbelief and War. Eemaan (Faith) was found in Madeenah, so Hijrah from the Land of Disbelief to the Land of Islaam became obligatory for those who were able to perform it. But when Makkah was conquered and it became a Land of Islaam, and the Arabs became Muslim, all of these lands became Lands of Islaam. This is why he said: **'There is no (more) Hijrah after the Conquest.'**

The aspect of a land being a Land of Disbelief, a Land of Belief or a Land of Sinners is not a permanent characteristic for each of these lands. Rather, it is a temporary characteristic that is dependent upon its inhabitants. So every land whose inhabitants are believers and dutiful to Allaah, that is a land of Allaah's allies at that (specific) time. And every land whose inhabitants are disbelievers, that is a land of disbelief at that (specific) time. And every land

---

[107] **Agreed Upon:** I have referenced it in *Irwaa-ul-Ghaleel* (1057)

[108] **Translator's Note:** Imaam Al-Albaanee counts the Hijrah his family made to Damascus, Syria when he was young as one of the blessings Allaah bestowed on him. He said: "Allaah has indeed bestowed many blessings on me, which I cannot even begin to count. Perhaps from the most important of them were two: The Hijrah my father made to Syria and his teaching me his trade of fixing watches. As for the first, it made learning Arabic easy for me. If we had stayed in Albania, I don't think I would have learned even one letter from it. And there is no way to the Book of Allaah and the Sunnah of His Messenger except through the path of the Arabic language." [*Hayaat-ul-'Alaamah al-Albaanee bi-Qalamihi* (pg. 5)]

whose inhabitants are sinners, that is a land of sinfulness at that (specific) time. But if people other than those whom we mentioned live in these lands thus transforming them due to the change of their inhabitants, then the land applies to those who currently reside there.

The same goes for a masjid if it is changed into a pub or it becomes a place of immorality or a place of wrong-doing or a church in which rivals are worshipped along with Allaah due to its inhabitants. Likewise with a pub or place of immorality, etc. - if it is turned into a masjid in which Allaah is worshipped alone, it becomes that way due to that. In the same manner, a pious man may become a sinner and a disbeliever may become a believer or a believer may become a disbeliever and so on - all in accordance to the changing of conditions from one state to another. Allaah says:

وَضَرَبَ اللَّهُ مَثَلًا قَرْيَةً كَانَتْ آمِنَةً مُّطْمَئِنَّةً

'And Allaah puts forth an example of a town that used to be safe and secure.' [Surah An-Nahl: 112]

This verse was revealed in Makkah when it was a Land of Disbelief, but yet in itself it was still the best of Allaah's lands and the most beloved to Him. Rather, what was intended in the *ayah* was the inhabitants (of Makkah). This is based on what At-Tirmidhee reported in *marfoo'* form, that the Prophet ﷺ said to Makkah while standing in Al-Hazwarah (a place in Makkah): **'By Allaah, you are indeed, the best of Allaah's lands and the most beloved of Allaah's lands to Allaah. And if it were not for the fact that my people expelled me from you, I would not have left.'** [109] And in another narration of the hadeeth, he ﷺ said: **'You are the best of Allaah's lands and the most beloved of Allaah's lands to me.'** [110]

So he ﷺ clarified that Makkah is the most beloved of Allaah's lands to Allaah and His Messenger ﷺ. In spite of this, his residing in Madeenah as well as that of those believers that resided there along with him was better than their residing in Makkah because of the fact that it was their place of migration (i.e. Hijrah)

---

[109] Its chain of narration is authentic. It is referenced in *Mishkaat-ul-Masaabeeh* (2725)
[110] Reported by Muslim and others, and it is referenced in *Irwaa-ul-Ghaleel* (1200)

This is why standing guard in the city's battle-posts is better than living in the vicinity of Makkah and Madeenah, as is authentically reported in the *Saheeh* from the Prophet ﷺ that he said: **'Standing guard in the battle-posts a day and a night for the sake of Allaah is better than fasting and performing the night prayer for one month. And whoever dies while standing guard at the battle-post dies a Mujaahid. His deeds will continue to flow and cause his sustenance to flow from Paradise. And he will be saved from the ones that bring about trials.'** [111]

In the *Sunan,* 'Uthmaan ﷺ reported that the Prophet ﷺ said: **'Standing guard at the battle-post one day for the sake of Allaah is better than one thousand days spent doing something else.'** And Abu Hurairah ﷺ said: **'That I spend a night standing guard at the battle-post for the sake of Allaah is more beloved to me than that I stand in prayer on the Night of Decree (*Laylat-ul-Qadar*) by the Black Stone.'** [112]

Based on this, the best land with respect to each individual is the land in which he is able to be the most obedient to Allaah and His Messenger. This varies according to the different conditions (of people). There is no specific land that is better for a person to reside in, per se; rather it is only **'better'** in accordance to each individual's dutifulness, obedience, submissiveness, and subservience to Allaah (while in that land).

Abud-Dardaa ﷺ wrote to Salmaan, saying: 'Come to the holy land!' So Salmaan wrote back to him: 'Indeed, the holy lands do not sanctify anyone. Rather it is only a person's deeds that sanctify him.' The Prophet ﷺ would make Salmaan and Abud-Dardaa associate with one another, and Salmaan was more knowledgeable than Abud-Dardaa in some aspects, amongst which was this one.

Allaah said to Moosaa:

سَأُرِيكُمْ دَارَ الْفَاسِقِينَ

[111] I say: At-Tirmidhee declared it sound (*hasan*), and Al-Haakim and Adh-Dhahabee authenticated it. I have referenced it in my comments to *al-Mukhtaarah* (no. 307)

[112] Rather, this report is raised (*marfoo'*) to a saying of the Prophet ﷺ. Ibn Hibbaan and others reported it like this with an authentic chain of narration. The references for it can be found in *as-Saheehah* (1068)

'I will show you the homeland of the sinful ones.' [Surah Al-A'raaf: 145]

This refers to the country in which those 'Amaaliqah used to live in. Then after this, it became a land of the believers. This is the land that the Qur'aan indicates as being the **'holy land'** and the land of Egypt that Allaah caused the Children of Israa'eel to inherit. Therefore, the conditions of countries are just like the conditions of people. A person can at times be either a Muslim, a disbeliever, a believer or a hypocrite. And at times he may be righteous and pious while at other times sinful and immoral.

This is the same case with places of residence with respect to their inhabitants. So a person's migration from a place of disbelief and sins to a place of Faith and obedience is just like his repenting and abandoning disbelief and sins for Faith and obedience. This is something that will remain until the Day of Judgement. Allaah says:

وَالَّذِينَ آمَنُوا مِن بَعْدُ وَهَاجَرُوا وَجَاهَدُوا مَعَكُمْ فَأُوْلَـئِكَ مِنكُمْ

'And those who believed afterwards and migrated and fought in Jihaad alongside you, they are of you.' [Surah Al-Anfaal: 75]

A group amongst the Salaf said: 'Anyone that migrates and strives hard (in Jihaad) up until the Day of Judgement falls under this *ayah*.' The same goes for Allaah's statement:

ثُمَّ إِنَّ رَبَّكَ لِلَّذِينَ هَاجَرُوا مِن بَعْدِ مَا فُتِنُوا ثُمَّ جَاهَدُوا وَصَبَرُوا إِنَّ رَبَّكَ مِن بَعْدِهَا لَغَفُورٌ رَّحِيمٌ

'Then verily your Lord - regarding those who migrated after they had been put to trials and thereafter fought in Jihaad and were patient - verily, your Lord, afterward, is Most Forgiving, Most Merciful.' [Surah An-Nahl: 110]

Those who fall under the meaning of this verse is everyone whose religion the Devil tests or causes to fall into sin, then abandons evil deeds and struggles against himself and others enemies, fights against the hypocrites by commanding the good and forbidding the evil, etc. and is patient with the statements and actions that befall him. And Allaah, Glorified and Exalted, knows best." [End of Ibn Taimiyyah's words]

I say: These are true facts and unique pearls from the knowledge of Shaikh-ul-Islaam Ibn Taimiyyah, may Allaah have mercy on him, which those speakers, authors and doctorate holders who reject Allaah's legislation are completely unaware of.

وَهُمْ يَحْسَبُونَ أَنَّهُمْ يُحْسِنُونَ صُنْعًا

"And yet they think they are doing something good!" [Surah Al-Kahf: 104]

So as a result (of this ignorance), they order the Palestinians to remain in their lands and forbid them from migrating from there. And yet they know that this will cause corruption to their religious and worldly affairs as well as destroy their men, dishonor their women, and lead their young boys and girls to go astray, as is frequently reported in the news about them due to the Jews' power over them and their raiding of their houses while the women are still sleeping in their beds! And this goes as well for all of the other tragedies and humiliations, which they are fully aware of, but yet disregard in the same manner as when a senseless ostrich pays no mind to a hunter! I feel sorry for them for they are truly ignorant, and they are unaware that they are ignorant. How can this not be so when they recite in the Qur'aan:

وَلَوْ أَنَّا كَتَبْنَا عَلَيْهِمْ أَنِ اقْتُلُوا أَنفُسَكُمْ أَوِ اخْرُجُوا مِن دِيَارِكُم مَّا فَعَلُوهُ إِلَّا قَلِيلٌ مِّنْهُمْ

"And had We prescribed upon them that: 'You should kill those from among yourselves (who are blameworthy)' or 'Leave from your homes', they would not do it except for a few amongst them." [Surah An-Nisaa: 66]

I wish I knew what they have to say about the Palestinians that have already left their lands, at times under the title of refugees and at other times under the title of immigrants. Will they say about them that they are sinners due to their claim that they left their lands for the Jews?! Of course! And what will they say about the millions of Afghanis that migrated from their country to Peshawar even though their country wasn't occupied by the Russians in the same manner as the Jews occupy Palestine today?!

And finally, what will they say about the Bosnians that sought asylum in recent times in some of the Islamic countries, amongst which is Jordan. Will they forbid them from leaving their country as well?? And will the head of calamities also say about them: "They are coming to us? What Are they doing here?!"

So he is also ignorant about Allaah's statement:

وَالَّذِينَ تَبَوَّؤُوا الدَّارَ وَالْإِيمَانَ مِن قَبْلِهِمْ يُحِبُّونَ مَنْ هَاجَرَ إِلَيْهِمْ وَلَا يَجِدُونَ فِي صُدُورِهِمْ حَاجَةً مِّمَّا أُوتُوا وَيُؤْثِرُونَ عَلَى أَنفُسِهِمْ وَلَوْ كَانَ بِهِمْ خَصَاصَةٌ

"And those who before them had homes (in Madeenah) and had adopted Faith - they love those who have migrated to them, and find no jealousy in their hearts for that which they have been given (from the war-booty), but rather give them preference over themselves even though they may have been in (more) need of it." [Surah Al-Hashr: 9]

Or perhaps they are as Allaah said about some of them:

يُحِلُّونَهُ عَامًا وَيُحَرِّمُونَهُ عَامًا

"They make it lawful one year and forbid it another year?!" [Surah At-Tawbah: 37]

"In time it will become clear to you what you used to be unaware of
When the one whom you least expected brings you the information."

[End of Al-Albaanee's words, may Allaah have mercy on him] [113]

[113] *Silsilat-ul-Ahaadeeth as-Saheehah* (vol. 6, part 2, pg. 848-855)

Appendix E: The Statement of Imaam 'Abdul-'Azeez bin 'Abdillaah bin Baaz [Died 1420H]

In his explanation of *Thalaathat-ul-Usool,* Imaam Ibn Baaz, may Allaah have mercy on him, said:

Then he ﷺ migrated to Madeenah after the harm of Quraysh grew too severe against him and his Companions. So Allaah allowed him to migrate from Makkah to Madeenah, to the Ansaar, due to the harm and oppression of the Quraysh. The Ansaar had given their pledge of allegiance to him ﷺ during the Hajj season on the understanding that he ﷺ would go to them and they would aid him, may Allaah be pleased with them. So when the oath of allegiance was completed and Allaah allowed him ﷺ to make Hijrah, he migrated to them.

Some of his Companions had already migrated before that to Abyssinia and lived with An-Najaashee for a while. So those among them who remained (i.e. in Makkah) migrated to Madeenah (with the Prophet). When he ﷺ settled down in Madeenah, the Companions that were in Abyssinia came to Madeenah and all of them settled there together, all praise be to Allaah.

So when he ﷺ settled in Madeenah, after having made Hijrah, Allaah commanded him with all of the remaining laws of Islaam, such as Zakaat, Fasting in Ramadaan, Pilgrimage to Allaah's House, Jihaad, and Commanding good and forbidding evil. This is since Madeenah had become a Land of Islaam. And it was the first capital of the Muslims.

They were commanded with these things since they were now able to command the good and forbid the evil. Thus it was from the Mercy of Allaah that He delayed these obligations until the Prophet ﷺ migrated to Madeenah. [114]

[114] Refer to his explanation of *Thalaathat-ul-Usool* (pg. 45-46) published by Daar ash-Sharee'ah, 2004. **Translator's Note:** This clearly shows that Hijrah is a door to good, since many of the obligatory acts came about after it.

Appendix F: The Statement of Imaam Muhammad bin Saalih Al-'Uthaimeen [Died 1421H]

In his explanation of *Thalaathat-ul-Usool*, Imaam Muhammad bin Saalih Al-'Uthaimeen, may Allaah have mercy on him, said:

Hijrah, according to the language, is derived from the word *hajr*, which means to abandon something. As for its religious meaning, then it is as the author defined it: "Moving from a Land of Shirk to a Land of Islaam." The Land of Shirk is a land in which the rites of Disbelief are established while the rites of Islaam, such as the Adhaan, praying in congregation, the 'Eid festivals and the Jumu'ah Prayer are not established in a general comprehensive manner. We only state here "a general comprehensive manner" so as to remove from this any land in which these rites are established in a restricted and limited manner, such as those disbelieving countries where Muslim minorities can be found, since a country does not become a Land of Islaam based on (some) Islamic rites that Muslim minorities establish there. As for the Land of Islaam, then it is a land in which these rites (of Islaam) are established in a general comprehensive manner.

Hijrah is obligatory upon every believer that is not able to openly practice his Religion while in a Land of Disbelief. His Islaam cannot become complete if he is not able to openly practice it unless he performs Hijrah. And that which is necessary for the completion of an obligation becomes itself obligatory.

The author states: "The proof for this is Allaah's saying: '**Verily, as for those whom the angels take (in death) while they are wronging themselves (by not performing Hijrah), they (angels) will say (to them): 'In what (condition) were you?' They will reply: 'We were weak and oppressed in the earth.' They (angels) will say: 'Was not the earth of Allaah spacious enough for you to migrate therein?' Such men will find their abode in Hell - what an evil destination! Except the weak ones among men, women and children - who cannot devise a plan, nor are they able to direct their way. These are the ones whom Allaah is (most) likely to forgive, and Allaah is Ever Oft-Pardoning, Most Forgiving.'** [Surah An-Nisaa: 97-99]"

There is proof in this *ayah* that those who did not migrate - even though they had the ability to make Hijrah - the angels will take them while reprimanding them and saying to them: **"Was not the earth of Allaah spacious enough for you to migrate therein?"** But as for those individuals who are from among the weak ones that are not able to perform Hijrah, Allaah has forgiven them due to their inability to do it. And Allaah does not burden a soul with more than it can handle.

The author continues: "And Allaah's saying: **'O My servants who believe (in Me)! Verily, My earth is spacious so to Me alone, perform your worship.'** [Surah Al-'Ankaboot: 56] Al-Baghawee, may Allaah have mercy on him, said: 'The reason for the revelation of this *ayah* was due to some Muslims who had resided in Makkah and did not migrate (to Madeenah). Allaah called out to them using the title of Eemaan (for them).'"

It appears that the author, may Allaah have mercy on him, is quoting this statement from Al-Baghawee based on its meaning (and not literally). This is if it is from his Tafseer, since this statement is not found in the Tafseer of Al-Baghawee with this wording.

The author continues: "The proof for Hijrah from the Sunnah is his ﷺ saying: **'Hijrah will not cease until repentance ceases. And repentance will not cease (to be accepted) until the sun rises from where it sets (i.e. the west).'**"

This is at the same time that all righteous deeds will cease to be accepted. Allaah says:

يَوْمَ يَأْتِي بَعْضُ آيَاتِ رَبِّكَ لَا يَنفَعُ نَفْسًا إِيمَانُهَا لَمْ تَكُنْ آمَنَتْ مِن قَبْلُ أَوْ كَسَبَتْ فِي إِيمَانِهَا خَيْرًا

"The Day that some of the signs of your Lord do come, no good will it do to a person to believe then, if he believed not before nor earned good through his Faith (i.e. by doing good deeds)." [Surah Al-An'aam: 158]

What is meant by **"some of the signs"** here is the sun rising from the west.

Now we will mention the ruling on traveling to the Lands of Disbelief. So we say: Traveling to the lands of the disbelievers is not permissible unless it meets three conditions:

The First Condition: The individual must have knowledge by which he can repel doubtful arguments.

The Second Condition: The individual must be practicing the Religion, which will prevent him from vain desires.

The Third Condition: He must have a (valid) need for going to those lands.

If these three conditions are not met, it is not permissible to travel to the lands of the disbelievers due to the *fitnah* (trials and afflictions) or the fear of *fitnah* that is found in that. It is also a waste of money since a person usually spends a lot of many in these kinds of trips. But as for the case where one is required to travel due to a necessity, such as medical treatment, acquiring some science that cannot be found in his own country, and he possesses knowledge and religion according to what we just described, then there is no harm in this. As for traveling to the lands of the disbelievers for tourism purposes, then this does not constitute a necessity. He may instead go to one of the Muslim countries whose inhabitants preserve the rites of Islaam. Furthermore, our country (i.e. Saudi Arabia) today, all praise be to Allaah, has become a country of tourism in some regions. So he may also go to one of these regions to spend his vacation time there.

As for residing permanently in the lands of the disbelievers, then this is very dangerous for the Religion, character, manners and etiquettes of a Muslim. I and others have witnessed first-hand the deviation of many people that resided in those lands. So they returned to their (Muslim) countries in a state different than how they left it. They came back as evil sinners, and some of them even came back having apostated from their religion, disbelieving in it as well as all of the (other) religions - and we seek refuge in Allaah from this! This is to the point that they have entered into absolute denial and rejection (i.e. agnosticism) and turned to mocking the Religion and its adherents, past and present.

Due to this, it is necessary, rather obligatory, to beware of this and to put forth conditions that will prevent one from falling into these destructive outcomes.

Therefore, residing in the Lands of Disbelief can only be done with the presence of two fundamental conditions:

The First Condition: The religion of the resident must be secure: This is such that the individual has with him such knowledge, Faith and firm resolve that will keep him firm upon his religion and cautious about deviating and diverting. He must also harbor enmity and hatred towards the disbelievers, keeping far away from befriending and loving them, for indeed befriending them and loving them is from the things that negates Faith in Allaah, as He says:

لَا تَجِدُ قَوْمًا يُؤْمِنُونَ بِاللَّهِ وَالْيَوْمِ الْآخِرِ يُوَادُّونَ مَنْ حَادَّ اللَّهَ وَرَسُولَهُ وَلَوْ كَانُوا آبَاءهُمْ أَوْ أَبْنَاءهُمْ أَوْ إِخْوَانَهُمْ أَوْ عَشِيرَتَهُمْ

"You will not find a people that believe in Allaah and the Last Day having love for those who oppose Allaah and His Messenger even if they be their fathers or their sons or their brothers or their kindred." [Surah Al-Mujaadilah: 22]

And Allaah says:

يَا أَيُّهَا الَّذِينَ آمَنُوا لاَ تَتَّخِذُوا الْيَهُودَ وَالنَّصَارَى أَوْلِيَاء بَعْضُهُمْ أَوْلِيَاء بَعْضٍ وَمَن يَتَوَلَّهُم مِّنكُمْ فَإِنَّهُ مِنْهُمْ إِنَّ اللّهَ لاَ يَهْدِي الْقَوْمَ الظَّالِمِينَ . فَتَرَى الَّذِينَ فِي قُلُوبِهِم مَّرَضٌ يُسَارِعُونَ فِيهِمْ يَقُولُونَ نَخْشَى أَن تُصِيبَنَا دَآئِرَةٌ فَعَسَى اللّهُ أَن يَأْتِيَ بِالْفَتْحِ أَوْ أَمْرٍ مِّنْ عِندِهِ فَيُصْبِحُوا عَلَى مَا أَسَرُّوا فِي أَنْفُسِهِمْ نَادِمِينَ

"O you who believe! Take not the Jews and the Christians as supporters. They are supporters of one other. And if any amongst you takes them as supporters, then surely he is one of them. Verily, Allaah does not guide a wrong-doing people. But you will see those in whose hearts is a disease (of hypocrisy) rushing to make alliances with them, saying: 'We only do

so for fear that some disaster may befall us.' Perhaps Allaah may bring a victory or a decision according to His Will. Then they will become regretful for what they have been keeping as a secret within themselves." [Surah Al-Maa'idah: 51-52]

It is also authentically reported in the *Saheeh* Collection that the Prophet ﷺ said that whoever loves a people is from among them, and that a man will be with he whom he loves. Having love for the enemies of Allaah is from the greatest dangers that a Muslim can fall into since loving them requires one to agree with them and follow them, or in the least fail to reject it. This is why the Prophet ﷺ said: **"Whoever loves a people is from among them."**

The Second Condition: The resident must be able to openly practice his Religion: This is such that he is able to establish the rites of Islaam without any restrictions. So he is not prevented from establishing the prayer, Jumu'ah prayer and the congregational prayers - if there is found someone else with him that can pray in congregation with him and establish the Jum'ah Prayer with him. Furthermore, he is not prevented from Zakaat, Fasting, Hajj and all of the other rites of the Religion. But if he is not able to do any of the above, it is not permissible for him to reside there due to Hijrah becoming obligatory on him at that point.

It is stated in *al-Mughnee* (8/457) concerning the discussion on the different categories people fall into with respect to Hijrah:

"**First:** This includes the one who it is obligatory upon and he is the one that has the ability to do it (i.e. perform Hijrah) while not being able to manifest his Religion in that land. Nor is he able to establish the obligatory requisites of his Religion due to his position of being in the midst of the disbelievers. This type of individual is obligated to make Hijrah due to Allaah statement: **'Verily, as for those whom the angels take (in death) while they are wronging themselves, they (angels) will say (to them): In what (condition) were you? They will reply: We were weak and oppressed on the earth. They (angels) will say: Was not the earth of Allaah spacious enough for you to migrate therein? Such men will find their abode in Hell - what an evil destination!'** [Surah An-Nisaa: 97] The severe threat that is mentioned in this *ayah* is proof for the obligation (of Hijrah). Also, establishing the obligatory aspects of one's Religion is an obligation in itself, for the one who is able to do that. And Hijrah is from the prerequisites of the obligatory and it is that which makes it complete. And whatever is essential for the completion of an obligation becomes itself obligatory."

After having met these two fundamental conditions, the aspect of residing in the lands of the disbelievers can be divided into several categories:

The First Category: That an individual resides there for the purpose of calling and encouraging people towards Islaam. This is a form of Jihaad. And it is a collective obligation on those who are able to do it, on the condition that they actually establish the Call and there can't be found anyone that prevents it or prevents people from accepting it. This is since Calling to Islaam is one of the obligations of the Religion, and it is the way of the Messengers. The Prophet ﷺ commanded us to convey from him in every time and place, as he ﷺ said: **"Convey from me even if it is one *ayah* (sign/verse)."**

The Second Category: That an individual resides there for the purpose of studying the conditions of the disbelievers and to gain understanding of their corrupt beliefs, false worship, immoral characters and disorganized behaviors, so that he can warn the people from being mesmerized by them and so that he can clarify the reality of their state of being to those who are beguiled by them. This type of residency is a form of Jihaad also, since the end result of it is to warn against disbelief and its people, which consists of an incitement towards Islaam and its guidance. This is since the corruption of disbelief is proof for the uprightness of Islaam, as the saying goes: "Things are made clear by their opposites."

However, this is only on the condition that he is able to achieve his intended goal without falling into an evil that is greater than it. So if he is not able to achieve his goal, such that, for example, he is prevented from spreading what they are upon and warning against it, then there is no benefit in his residing there. And if he is able to achieve his goal while at the same time falling into a greater evil, such as the people reacting to his actions by reviling Islaam, the Messenger of Islaam and the Imaams of Islaam, then he is obligated to refrain from it based on Allaah's statement:

وَلَا تَسُبُّوا الَّذِينَ يَدْعُونَ مِن دُونِ اللَّهِ فَيَسُبُّوا اللَّهَ عَدْوًا بِغَيْرِ عِلْمٍ كَذَٰلِكَ زَيَّنَّا لِكُلِّ أُمَّةٍ عَمَلَهُمْ ثُمَّ إِلَىٰ رَبِّهِم مَّرْجِعُهُمْ فَيُنَبِّئُهُم بِمَا كَانُوا يَعْمَلُونَ

"And insult not those whom they (i.e. the polytheists) worship besides Allaah, lest they insult Allaah wrongfully without knowledge. Thus have We beautified to every nation its actions. Then to their Lord is their return and He shall inform them of what they used to do." [Surah Al-An'aam: 108]

Similar to this is when an individual goes to reside in the Lands of Disbelief in order to assist the Muslims against the evil plots (of the disbelievers), by warning the Muslims about them, as was the case when the Prophet ﷺ sent Hudhaifah bin Al-Yamaan ؓ to the pagan Arabs during the Battle of the Trench so that he could gain information about them.

The Third Category: That he resides there due to the requirement of a Muslim country and in order to administer its relations with the disbelieving countries, as is the case with the employees found in embassies. The ruling on these embassies is the same ruling as those who reside there because of it (i.e. to work there). So, for example, the cultural attaché may reside (in the lands of the disbelievers) in order to administer the affairs of the students, monitor them and encourage them to adhere to the religious aspects, morals and manners of Islaam. So a great benefit is achieved and a great evil is repelled as a result of his residing there.

The Fourth Category: That he resides there for a specific need that is allowable, such as business and medical treatment. It is allowed to reside there in accordance with the need. The people of knowledge, may Allaah have mercy on them, have issued statements concerning the permissibility of entering the Lands of Disbelief for the sake of business, quoting narrations about that from some of the Companions.

The Fifth Category: That he resides there for the purpose of studying. This falls under the same type as the category just mentioned before - residing due to a specific need - however it is more dangerous and more destructive to the religion and morals of the resident. This is since a student usually considers himself to be in a lower position than that of his teachers. So this results in his admiration for them and his contentment with their views, ideas and manners, thus causing him to blind-follow them, except for those whom Allaah has willed to protect, and they are few.

Furthermore, a student usually feels like he is need of his teacher. So this leads him to have love for him and to outwardly praise him in that which he is upon from deviation and misguidance. A student also has colleagues in his place of study from which he will take some of them as friends, loving them, supporting them and being influenced by them. Due to the danger of this category, it is an obligation on the individual to be more cautious about this aspect than those mentioned before it. In addition to the two primary conditions, it is also necessary to meet the following conditions for this category:

The First Condition: The student must be at an advanced level of intellectual maturity by which he can distinguish between what is beneficial and what is harmful and by which he can see far into the distant future. As for sending novices, "young in age", and those who possess inferior intellects, then this also poses great danger to their religion, character and behavior. Furthermore, this poses great danger to the nations that they will return back to and to whom they will unleash the poisons that they consumed from those disbelievers, as reality has and continues to bear witness to. Many of those who were sent (to disbelieving lands) came back different from how they left. They came back with deviations in their religion, manners and behavior, and great harm befell them and their communities as a result of this, as is known and witnessed. Sending these types of people (to the lands of the disbelievers) is the same as presenting female sheep to ferocious dogs.

The Second Condition: The student must have sufficient knowledge of the religion that enables him to distinguish the truth from falsehood and to fight against the falsehood with the truth so that he won't be deceived by their falsehood, thinking it to be the truth, having it be obscure to him, or unable to repel it, thus leaving him confused or following falsehood. In a supplication reported in the narrations, it states: **"O Allaah, show me the truth as true and enable me to follow it. And show me the falsehood as false and enable me to avoid it. And do not make it obscure to me, thus causing me to go astray."**

The Third Condition: The student must possess sufficient religious qualities that will protect him and fortify him from disbelief and sinfulness. Therefore, one who is weak in his religion is not safe in residing there, unless Allaah wills. This is due to the strength of the attacker and the weakness of the defender. The means of disbelief and sinfulness are strong, many and vary. So if they fall upon a place that has weak defenses, its effect will take its toll.

The Fourth Condition: There must be a valid need for the knowledge that he is residing in those lands to acquire, such as there being a benefit to the Muslims in learning it, and nothing like it can be found in the schools in his own country. But if it is from the extracurricular forms of knowledge that serves no benefit to the Muslims or knowledge of it can be acquired in other Muslim countries, it is not permissible for him to reside in the Lands of Disbelief for that purpose due to the danger that will befall the individual's religion and manners and due to his spending lots of money for no beneficial purpose.

The Sixth Category: That he resides there for the purpose of living there. This is more dangerous than all the categories before it and graver due to the evils that will result from his complete and total assimilation with the people of disbelief. It is also due to the fact that he will feel that he is a citizen of that country and thus required to be like the rest of the citizens in terms of their love, support and adding to the ranks of the disbelievers. He will also have to raise his family amongst the disbelievers, so they will be influenced by their manners and customs. And perhaps they may imitate them in their beliefs and rituals.

This is why the Prophet ﷺ said in a hadeeth: **"Whoever has intimate ties with a polytheist and resides with him, then he is like him."** Even though the chain of narration of this hadeeth is weak, it still has a point since residing in a place leads to participating (in that place's community). Qays bin Haazim reported that Jareer bin 'Abdillaah ﷺ narrated that the Prophet ﷺ said: **"I am free from every Muslim that resides amongst the polytheists."** They said: "O Messenger of Allaah, why?" He said: **"Their fires should not be visible to one another."** [Reported by Abu Dawood and At-Tirmidhee] Most of the narrators reported it in *mursal* form from

Qays bin Haazim from the Prophet ﷺ.[115] At-Tirmidhee said: "I heard Muhammad, i.e. Al-Bukhaaree, say: 'What is correct is that the hadeeth of Qays from the Prophet ﷺ is *mursal*.'"

How can a believing soul be content with living in the Lands of the Disbelievers in which the rites of disbelief are openly proclaimed and the rule used to govern there is other than that of Allaah and His Messenger, while he witnesses this with his own eyes and hears it with his own ears and is pleased with it? Rather, he ascribes himself to that country and lives in it with his wife and children, feeling at ease there just as he would feel at ease in the Lands of the Muslims in spite of the great danger found in that for the religion and manners of himself, his wife and his children.

This is the last of what we have reached regarding the ruling on residing in the Lands of Disbelief. We ask Allaah to make it in conformity with what is true and correct. [116]

---

[115] **Translator's Note:** Meaning a Taabi'ee reporting from the Prophet without a Companion in between.

[116] Refer to *Jaami' Shurooh al-Usool–uth-Thalaathah* (pg. 758-764)

Appendix G: The Statement of Imaam Muqbil bin Haadee Al-Waadi'ee [Died 1422H]

Question: There is a French brother that lives with his mother and brother. He is the only one in his family who has accepted Islaam. His father was a Christian and he died upon his Christian beliefs. His mother is Jewish and his brother is a disbeliever. However, his brother also wishes to leave from home. So is it required for this Muslim son to make Hijrah and leave the Land of Disbelief, fleeing for the sake of his Religion, while leaving his mother all alone?

Answer: The question is about a brother that accepted Islaam whilst living amongst a disbelieving family. So his father was a Christian who died upon his Christian beliefs, his mother is Jewish and his brother is a disbeliever. So how should his interactions be with his mother.

His interactions with her must be according to the limits of the Book and the Sunnah, as Allaah says in His Noble Book concerning polytheist parents:

وَصَاحِبْهُمَا فِي الدُّنْيَا مَعْرُوفًا

"And accompany them in the worldly life upon goodness." [Surah Luqmaan: 15]

He also says in His Noble Book:

لَا تَجِدُ قَوْمًا يُؤْمِنُونَ بِاللَّهِ وَالْيَوْمِ الْآخِرِ يُوَادُّونَ مَنْ حَادَّ اللَّهَ وَرَسُولَهُ وَلَوْ كَانُوا آبَاءَهُمْ أَوْ أَبْنَاءَهُمْ أَوْ إِخْوَانَهُمْ أَوْ عَشِيرَتَهُمْ

"You will not find any people who believe in Allaah and the Last Day making friendship with those who oppose Allaah and His Messenger, even if they are their fathers or their sons or their brothers or their kindred." [Surah Al-Mujaadilah: 22]

And He says:

يَا أَيُّهَا الَّذِينَ آمَنُوا لَا تَتَّخِذُوا آبَاءكُمْ وَإِخْوَانَكُمْ أَوْلِيَاء إَنِ اسْتَحَبُّوا الْكُفْرَ عَلَى الإِيمَانِ وَمَن يَتَوَلَّهُم مِّنكُمْ فَأُوْلَـئِكَ هُمُ الظَّالِمُونَ

"O you who believe, take not your fathers and your brothers as supporters if they prefer disbelief over Faith. And whoever of you does so, then he is one of the wrong-doers." [Surah At-Tawbah: 23]

So he must treat his mother with kindness for as long as he is with her. But he must not compromise any part of his Religion while doing this. He should also hold hatred for her because of the fact that she is a disbeliever. But if his soul insists on loving her - and this is a natural type of love - then Allaah willing there is no sin upon him. When the Prophet ﷺ called Abu Taalib to Islaam, and Abu Taalin refused to become Muslim, Allaah said:

إِنَّكَ لَا تَهْدِي مَنْ أَحْبَبْتَ وَلَكِنَّ اللَّهَ يَهْدِي مَن يَشَاء

"Verily, you cannot guide those whom you love, but rather, it is Allaah who guides whoever He wills." [Surah Al-Qasas: 56]

We can derive from the *ayah* two possible meanings. It can mean "those whom you love." This is one possibility. As for the other possibility, then it could mean: "you cannot guide those whom you would love to be guided." This is closer to correctness since he didn't love for him to be guided more than others except due to his closeness to him. This is as Al-Miqdaad bin Al-Aswad ﷺ said: "One of us would become Muslim and see his father remain a disbeliever or his mother a disbeliever or his relative, and so he would not live happily, since that person would die upon disbelief and enter the Hellfire."

Allaah, Mighty and Sublime, said to His Prophet ﷺ:

وَأَنذِرْ عَشِيرَتَكَ الْأَقْرَبِينَ

"And warn your close relatives." [Surah Ash-Shu'araa: 214]

The Prophet ﷺ once climbed Safaa and said: **"O gathering of Quraysh, O Banee 'Abd Manaaf, O Banee Haashim."** He called all of Quraysh and warned them.

So it is upon this brother to sincerely advise them. However, the true guidance that Allaah admits into the hearts – that is for Allaah alone, as He says:

لَيْسَ عَلَيْكَ هُدَاهُمْ وَلَـكِنَّ اللّهَ يَهْدِي مَن يَشَاء

"Their guidance is not upon you, but rather, Allaah guides whom He wills." [Surah Al-Baqarah: 272]

And Allaah said about His Prophet ﷺ:

وَإِنَّكَ لَتَهْدِي إِلَى صِرَاطٍ مُّسْتَقِيمٍ

"And verily, you guide to a Straight Path." [Surah Ash-Shooraa: 52]

This means: "You direct the people to the Straight Path." But as for the guidance that Allaah places in the heart, then this is only for Allaah.

As for him leaving his mother and the Land of Disbelief and departing from his country, fleeing for the sake of his Religion, then if he fears that trials will befall him, he should present Islaam to his mother. If she becomes Muslim, then that is good, but if not, then there is no harm. Rather, he is obligated to migrate, as Allaah says in His Noble Book:

إِنَّ الَّذِينَ تَوَفَّاهُمُ الْمَلآئِكَةُ ظَالِمِي أَنْفُسِهِمْ قَالُوا فِيمَ كُنتُمْ قَالُوا كُنَّا مُسْتَضْعَفِينَ فِي الأَرْضِ قَالْوَاْ أَلَمْ تَكُنْ أَرْضُ اللّهِ وَاسِعَةً فَتُهَاجِرُواْ فِيهَا فَأُوْلَـئِكَ مَأْوَاهُمْ جَهَنَّمُ وَسَاءتْ مَصِيرًا . إِلاَّ الْمُسْتَضْعَفِينَ مِنَ الرِّجَالِ وَالنِّسَاء وَالْوِلْدَانِ لاَ يَسْتَطِيعُونَ حِيلَةً وَلاَ يَهْتَدُونَ سَبِيلاً

"Verily, as for those whom the angels take (in death) while they are wronging themselves (by not performing Hijrah), they (angels) will say (to them): 'In what (condition) were you?' They will reply: 'We were

weak and oppressed in the earth.' They (angels) will say: 'Was not the earth of Allaah spacious enough for you to migrate therein?' Such men will find their abode in Hell – what an evil destination! Except the weak ones among men, women and children who cannot devise a plan, nor are they able to find a way (to make Hijrah)." [Surah An-Nisaa: 97-98]

And He says:

قُلْ إِن كَانَ آبَاؤُكُمْ وَأَبْنَآؤُكُمْ وَإِخْوَانُكُمْ وَأَزْوَاجُكُمْ وَعَشِيرَتُكُمْ وَأَمْوَالٌ اقْتَرَفْتُمُوهَا وَتِجَارَةٌ تَخْشَوْنَ كَسَادَهَا وَمَسَاكِنُ تَرْضَوْنَهَا أَحَبَّ إِلَيْكُم مِّنَ اللّهِ وَرَسُولِهِ وَجِهَادٍ فِي سَبِيلِهِ فَتَرَبَّصُوا حَتَّى يَأْتِيَ اللّهُ بِأَمْرِهِ وَاللّهُ لاَ يَهْدِي الْقَوْمَ الْفَاسِقِينَ

"Say: If your fathers, your sons, your brothers, your wives, your kindred, the wealth that you have gained, the commerce in which you fear a decline, and the dwellings in which you delight are dearer to you than Allaah and His Messenger, and striving hard and fighting in His Cause, then wait until Allaah brings about His decision (torment). And Allaah guides not the people who are disobedient." [Surah At-Tawbah: 24] [117]

Question: One of the brothers traveled abroad in order to seek religious knowledge and he left behind his mother. After being gone for a while, she asked him to come back because she missed him. But she is not Muslim. So should he obey her request?

Answer: Yes, he should obey her request, since the Lord of Might says in his Noble Book:

وَصَاحِبْهُمَا فِي الدُّنْيَا مَعْرُوفًا

"And accompany them in the worldly life upon goodness." [Surah Luqmaan: 15]

But in the event that he doesn't have the ability or any way to go back, then Allaah does not burden a soul with more than it can handle. Nevertheless,

[117] *Tuhfat-ul-Mujeeb* (pg. 261-263)

he should still communicate with her via telephone or through correspondence. [118]

Question: What is the ruling on migrating from a Land of Disbelief to a Land of Islaam? And what should the one who doesn't have the ability to migrate do, knowing that there are some places in America that are less evil than other places?

Answer: We advise the brothers, if they are able to, to travel to one of the mountain areas and reside there in order to preserve their families and children. This is since the Prophet ﷺ said: **"Every individual is born upon the state of *Fitrah* (pure natural inclination). But it is his parents that make him a Jew or a Christian or a Zoroastrian."**

Migrating to the Lands of the Muslims is very burdensome. Perhaps you may arrive at a (Muslim) country and they consider you to be a spy and thus return you back to where you came from. Corruption can also be found in all of the Muslim lands - whether in small amounts or large amounts.

Therefore, I say: The one who is upright in his Religion - regardless of whether he lives in America or in another country - and is unable and incapable of performing Hijrah, there is no sin upon him, if Allaah wills. But if he feels that he is able to and capable of making Hijrah, then I advise him to leave his children and wife behind so that he can go and look into the prospective country - is it right for living? And is he able to reside there or will they require him to get residency documents and other things that he cannot get? Allaah does not burden a soul with more than it can handle. And Allaah does not burden a soul with something except that He has given it the ability to endure it.

Hijrah is in effect until the Day of Judgement: **"Verily, as for those whom the angels take (in death) while they are wronging themselves (by not performing Hijrah), they (angels) will say (to them): 'In what (condition) were you?' They will reply: 'We were weak and oppressed in the earth.' They (angels) will say: 'Was not the earth of Allaah spacious enough for you to migrate therein?' Such men will find their abode in Hell - what an**

---

[118] *Tuhfat-ul-Mujeeb* (pg. 129); Translator's Note: This question was presented to the Shaikh from someone in America.

evil destination! Except the weak ones among men, women and children who cannot devise a plan, nor are they able to find a way (to make Hijrah)." [Surah An-Nisaa: 97-98] [119]

Question: What is the status of the hadeeth: **"Verily, when the polytheist becomes Muslim, Allaah does not accept any deed from him until he migrates to a Land of Islaam?"**

Answer: This has been reported from the Prophet ﷺ regarding Hijrah. A Bedouin Arab once came to the Prophet ﷺ and asked him about Hijrah, so he said: **"Woe to you, indeed Hijrah is a serious matter. Do you have any camels?"** He said: "Yes." He ﷺ said: **"Do you pay Zakaat on them?"** He said: "Yes." He ﷺ said: **"Do you give anything out from them?"** He said: "Yes." He ﷺ said: **"So you milk them on the day that they go to the watering ground?"** He said: "Yes." He ﷺ said: **"So do deeds from behind the sea, for indeed Allaah will never cause any of your deeds to go to waste."**

Not all of the Companions made Hijrah. Rather, sometimes a man would come to the Prophet ﷺ and he would order him to go back to his people, as occurs in the story of 'Amr bin 'Abasah when he came to the Prophet ﷺ and told him that he wanted to be with him. So he ﷺ said: **"Verily, you will not be able to on this day of yours. Did you not see my condition and the condition of the people? Rather, go back to your people. But when you become aware that I have appeared, then come to me."** So he went to him (later) in Madeenah.

An individual may migrate and encounter conflicts and see evil things transpiring. So perhaps he may see theft, indecent female exposure, unveiling, bribery, interest-based banks, enmity between Muslims, chasing after the worldly life with greed, deception, and lies, and think that this is Islaam, whereas Islaam is free from this. Islaam has forbidden and rejected all of these things. And if we were to list the evidences for that, the talk would be prolonged. Rather, it is those with weak Faith that are the ones who perpetrate these crimes. [120]

---

[119] *Tuhfat-ul-Mujeeb* (pg. 134-135)
[120] *Tuhfat-ul-Mujeeb* (pg. 136-137)

Question: Is Hijrah from the Land of Disbelief to the Land of Islaam still in effect?

Answer: The Prophet ﷺ said: **"Hijrah will not cease until repentance ceases (to be accepted). And repentance will not cease (to be accepted) until the sun rises from where it sets."**

And the Prophet ﷺ said: **"There is no (more) Hijrah after the Conquest, but rather Jihaad and (good) intention."**

What is meant by this is Hijrah from Makkah, since it had become a Land of Islaam. But as for (regular) Hijrah, then it is ongoing even if there is nothing (i.e. proofs for it) except for Allaah's statement:

إِنَّ الَّذِينَ تَوَفَّاهُمُ الْمَلاَئِكَةُ ظَالِمِي أَنْفُسِهِمْ قَالُوا فِيمَ كُنتُمْ قَالُوا كُنَّا
مُسْتَضْعَفِينَ فِي الأَرْضِ قَالُوَا أَلَمْ تَكُنْ أَرْضُ اللهِ وَاسِعَةً فَتُهَاجِرُوا فِيهَا
فَأُوْلَـئِكَ مَأْوَاهُمْ جَهَنَّمُ وَسَاءتْ مَصِيرًا . إِلاَّ الْمُسْتَضْعَفِينَ مِنَ الرِّجَالِ
وَالنِّسَاء وَالْوِلْدَانِ لاَ يَسْتَطِيعُونَ حِيلَةً وَلاَ يَهْتَدُونَ سَبِيلاً

"Verily, as for those whom the angels take (in death) while they are wronging themselves (by not performing Hijrah), they (angels) will say (to them): 'In what (condition) were you?' They will reply: 'We were weak and oppressed in the earth.' They (angels) will say: 'Was not the earth of Allaah spacious enough for you to migrate therein?' Such men will find their abode in Hell – what an evil destination! Except the weak ones among men, women and children who cannot devise a plan, nor are they able to find a way (to make Hijrah). [Surah An-Nisaa: 97-98]

The reason why this *ayah* was revealed is stated in the *Saheeh* from 'Ikrimah on Ibn 'Abbaas that a group of people among the Muslims used to be in Makkah, so they went out to fight alongside the pagan Arabs in the Battle of Badr. Among them were those who were forced to go out to fight (against the Muslims) and they were killed. The Prophet ﷺ was asked about them, so Allaah revealed this (above) *ayah*. Therefore, migrating from the Lands of Disbelief to the Lands of Islaam will continue to be obligatory until the Final Hour is established.

So now there remains the following question: "Where should one migrate to? Should he migrate to the *Haramain* (i.e. Makkah and Madeenah)? Will he be accepted there or not?"

There are some people that will accept him and others who will not accept him. And it is possible that he will be sent back (to his country of origin). Or he might migrate to Yemen where they may give him three months to stay there. So after three months he has to pay a 20 riyal fine for every day he overstays, and so on and so forth. Therefore, ask Allaah to send the Muslims a Land of Hijrah where they can migrate to. [121]

Question: What is your view on migrating to a Land of Disbelief, i.e. from a Land of Islaam to a Land of Disbelief? Should we abide by the three excuses mentioned by Al-Haafidh Ibn Hajr in *Fat'h-ul-Baaree* and act in accordance to their requisites even though they contradict some of the authentic texts, as I believe, and Allaah knows best, or must we abide by what is apparent from the texts and follow what some of the scholars have ruled on this issue – that its being permissible (to reside in a Land of Disbelief) is not acceptable? Amongst the texts (that prohibit residing in the Land of Disbelief) is that which the Three have reported, and its chain of narration is authentic on the authority of Jareer ﷺ, that he said: "The Messenger of Allaah ﷺ said: **'I am free from every Muslim that resides amongst the polytheists.'"**

And Samurah bin Jundub ﷺ reported that the Messenger of Allaah ﷺ said: **"Whoever neighbors a polytheist and lives with him, then he is (just) like him."** [Reported by Abu Dawood]

Jareer bin 'Abdillaah ﷺ reported that Allaah's Messenger ﷺ once sent a military detachment to Kath'am where they found a people that had sought refuge in prostration, but yet were killed hastily. When news of this reached the Prophet ﷺ, he ordered that half the blood-money be paid for them and said: **"I am free from every Muslim that resides amongst the polytheists."** They said: "Why is that, O Messenger of Allaah?" He ﷺ said: **"Their two fires should not be visible to one another."** [Reported by Abu Dawood and At-Tirmidhee]

---

[121] *Ijaabat-us-Saa'il 'alaa Ahamm-il-Masaa'il* (pg. 615-616)

I would like for you to explain the issue to us in detail and clarify to us the way to achieve absolvement from these doubts, amongst which is: (Choosing between) remaining in Australia in order to seek family income or returning to Algeria where the country is not governed by the laws of Islaam, as you are aware, even though most of the people there are Muslims that adhere to Islaam.

Answer: All praise is for Allaah. Lord of the worlds, and may the praises and peace of Allaah be on our prophet, Muhammad, his family and all of his Companions. I bear witness that there is no deity that has the right to be worshipped except Allaah - alone and with no partner, and I bear witness that Muhammad is His slave and messenger. To proceed:

Hijrah will remain legislated until the sun rises from its place of setting (i.e. the west). Hijrah can either occur from the Lands of Disbelief to the Lands of Islaam or from the Lands of Fear to the Lands of Security. This second category is clear from the migration that took place by some of the Companions to Abyssinia, since they migrated from Makkah, as is reported in the *Saheeh*, to Abyssinia. At that time, Makkah was a Land of Disbelief, as well as a Land of Fear and Insecurity, while Abyssinia was a Land of Peace and Security. Our Prophet Muhammad ﷺ told his Companions, or he advised them, to migrate to Abyssinia, saying to them: **"There is a king there that does not oppress those who live in his kingdom."**

As for the *ahaadeeth* that the brother mentioned, then let us begin by discussing them. The hadeeth of Jareer bin 'Abdillaah Al-Bajlee رضي الله عنه was reported by Abu Dawood and At-Tirmidhee who both confirmed its *Irsaal*, i.e. that it is from the path of Ismaa'eel bin Abee Khaalid from Qays bin Abee Haazim from the Prophet ﷺ. As for the hadeeth of Samurah رضي الله عنه, Al-Haakim authenticated it while Adh-Dhahabee commented on it saying that it had an obscure chain of narration. And it is just as he said, since there are unknown narrators in it.

So therefore the two hadeeths that indicate that it is not permissible for a Muslim to reside in a Land of Disbelief are both weak narrations, hence they cannot be used as evidence. What remains is Allaah's statement: **"Verily, as for those whom the angels take (in death) while they are wronging themselves (by not performing Hijrah), they (angels) will say (to them): 'In what (condition) were you?' They will reply: 'We were**

weak and oppressed in the earth.' They (angels) will say: 'Was not the earth of Allaah spacious enough for you to migrate therein?' Such men will find their abode in Hell – what an evil destination! Except the weak ones among men, women and children – who cannot devise a plan, nor are they able to direct their way." [Surah An-Nisaa: 97-98]

So whoever migrates or goes to a (disbelieving) country, and then joins their ranks or is called to join their ranks for fighting, then he is from among them. Even though he is not a disbeliever like them, he is still considered a sinner whom it is permissible to kill.

It has been mentioned in the *Saheeh* Collection that once the Prophet ﷺ was asked by his Companions about coming upon a people for battle at night and not being able to distinguish between men, women, children and those who don't fight inside the houses, so he ﷺ said: **"They are from them."**

Therefore, I advise those who are forced to go to a Land of Disbelief (due to an emergency) to make it their intention to call (the people there) to Allaah, and they should not deviate from that goal afterward. There is another restriction, which is that when an individual intends to make Hijrah, it is not lawful for him to go back to the country from where he migrated. This is even if Allaah punishes the tyrants, straightens things out, and establishes peace and security in the land that the individual migrated from.

If he plans to return back to the country from where he migrated (in the future), he should then intend by his travel a temporary absence and not Hijrah. But if he makes it his intention to go there for the purpose of Da'wah (i.e. Calling to Allaah), then this is also good. Our proof for this is what has been reported in the two *Saheeh* Collections that Sa'ad bin Abee Waqqaas ﷺ once complained to the Messenger of Allaah ﷺ stating that he was afraid to die in Makkah, i.e. the place where he had migrated from. So the Prophet ﷺ said to him: **"And perhaps you will have a long life so that some people will be benefited by you while others will be harmed by you."** However, the unfortunate one was Sa'ad bin Khawlah. The Prophet ﷺ felt sorry for him that he died while in Makkah. Sa'ad bin Khawlah had migrated from the people of Makkah and went to Madeenah, but then returned to Makkah - not as a result of apostasy - and died there. So the Prophet ﷺ said: **"However, the unfortunate one is Sa'ad bin Khawlah."** [122]

The Prophet ﷺ felt sorry for him that he died in Makkah. It seems that this is from the statements of Az-Zuhree. Furthermore, during the Farewell Pilgrimage, the Prophet ﷺ did not allow any of those who had migrated to Madeenah to remain in Makkah for more than three days. It has been reported in a hadeeth, of which there is speculation concerning its chain of narration, that the Prophet ﷺ mentioned some Bedouins that apostated after having made Hijrah or something with this meaning. This was reported by Ibn Mas'ood ﷺ. But one should investigate into its chain of narration.

These two hadeeths are sufficient. Therefore, an individual can either intend to flee for the sake of his Religion from calamities (*fitan*) or he can intend to go there for the purpose of Calling to Allaah (Da'wah), and there is no harm in him gaining a skill while living there.

But as for his going there with the intention that he is migrating from a Land of Islaam to a Land of Disbelief, then in reality, the definition of an emigrant (*Muhaajir*) doesn't apply to him. Hijrah linguistically means to abandon something. So can he honestly intend to abandon his country, even if security becomes established there and ruling by what Allaah has revealed returns back to that country? He can't intend this. This is from a linguistic standpoint. As for its religious definition, Hijrah means to flee from a Land of Disbelief to a Land of Islaam or from a Land of Corruption to a Land of Rectification. This does not apply to what the brother, may Allaah preserve him, mentioned. So he should make it his intention, if Allaah wills, to call to Allaah, and there is not harm if he seeks to gain a skill or profession while living there.

---

[122] **Translator's Note:** This event occurred during the Prophet's Farewell Pilgrimage, when he and his Companions who had migrated to Madeenah returned to their homeland of Makkah for Hajj. There, Sa'ad bin Abee Waqqaas ﷺ fell terribly ill and feared he would die in Makkah – something he hated since he had already migrated to Madeenah. The Prophet ﷺ cleared him and informed him that the unfortunate one was Sa'ad bin Khawlah for he had migrated to Madeenah, returned to Makkah, and then died there. Sa'ad bin Abee Waqqaas eventually recovered and outlived the Prophet ﷺ.

This is also on the condition that he doesn't ally himself with the disbelievers, for Allaah says in His Noble Book:

يَا أَيُّهَا الَّذِينَ آمَنُوا لاَ تَتَّخِذُوا الْيَهُودَ وَالنَّصَارَى أَوْلِيَاء بَعْضُهُمْ أَوْلِيَاء بَعْضٍ وَمَن يَتَوَلَّهُم مِّنكُمْ فَإِنَّهُ مِنْهُمْ إِنَّ اللّهَ لاَ يَهْدِي الْقَوْمَ الظَّالِمِينَ

"O you who believe, do not take the Jews and the Christians as supporters. They are allies of one another. And whoever allies himself with them, then he is among them. Verily, Allaah does not guide the wrong-doing people." [Surah Al-Maa'idah: 51]

So when a Muslim travels to these countries, he should not - rather he must not - ally himself with or support the enemies of Islaam. And he must not advise them unless it is to call them to Allaah and to the Sunnah of the Messenger of Allaah ﷺ. He should advise them to take hold of that which will benefit them - and that is embracing the Religion of Islaam. It is not permissible for him to belittle Islaam while in those countries, as this is unlawful. Allaah says in His Noble Book:

وَلِلَّهِ الْعِزَّةُ وَلِرَسُولِهِ وَلِلْمُؤْمِنِينَ

"And to Allaah belongs the honor and (also) to His Messenger and the believers." [Surah Al-Munaafiqoon: 8]

And He says:

بَشِّرِ الْمُنَافِقِينَ بِأَنَّ لَهُمْ عَذَابًا أَلِيمًا . الَّذِينَ يَتَّخِذُونَ الْكَافِرِينَ أَوْلِيَاء مِن دُونِ الْمُؤْمِنِينَ أَيَبْتَغُونَ عِندَهُمُ الْعِزَّةَ فَإِنَّ العِزَّةَ لِلّهِ جَمِيعًا

"Give tidings to the hypocrites that for them will be a painful torment - those who take the disbelievers as allies instead of the believers. Do they seek honor from them? For indeed, all the honor belongs to Allaah." [Surah An-Nisaa: 138-139]

So the glory and honor belongs to Allaah, His Messenger and the believers. As for an individual having to go and belittle Islaam in front of these people, then the earth of Allaah is spacious. It is possible for him to go to any Islamic country and establish his Islaam there. And if the Muslim countries have become such that they do not assist the person that migrates to them, instead making things difficult for him such as requiring him to provide visas, residency papers, saying this person is a foreigner and this belongs to us and so on and so forth, this is something for which Allaah sent down no authority. When the Companions migrated from Makkah to Madeenah, the Ansaar received them with the warmest of welcomes.

It is reported in the two *Saheehs* from Anas ﷺ and 'Abdur-Rahmaan bin 'Awf ﷺ that Sa'ad bin Ar-Rabee' - who was from the Ansaar - said to 'Abdur-Rahmaan bin 'Awf - who was from the Muhaajireen - when he came to Makkah: **"Choose one of my (two) wives so that I may her divorce her for you. And I wish to split my wealth in half with you."** At this, 'Abdur-Rahmaan bin 'Awf said: **"May Allaah bless you with regard to your family and wealth. Just show me where the marketplace is."**

This was the condition of the Companions of Allaah's Messenger ﷺ and the condition of our Pious Predecessors. They would love those who migrated to them and they would not find any jealousy in their hearts for that which they had been bestowed, giving them preference over themselves even though they had a greater need (for assistance). [123]

In spite of this, we must be patient with the Muslims and with the Muslim rulers, and we must flee from the Lands of Disbelief to the Lands of Islaam. If we are compelled to go to a Land of Disbelief, we should fear Allaah with regard to our Islaam for indeed many Muslims that travel to America, Britain, Germany or one of the other disbelieving countries serve as barriers for some Christians, atheists and Jews. They serve as obstacles between them and Islaam. This is due to the fact that these Muslims do not practice Islaam. A Muslim is prohibited from selling alcohol, but yet he sells it. He is prohibited from selling pork, but yet he sells its meat and so on. He is forbidden from doing many things, such as stealing and treachery, but yet he doesn't act upon Islaam.

In fact, he may even have worse conduct than the Jews and Christians. So these kinds of people give Islaam a bad reputation, even though Islaam is free from them. This is even the case with us, even though we fall short in

---

[123] See Surah Al-Hashr: 9

acting upon Islaam, Islaam is still Islaam – it is a proof against us and we are not a proof against it.

The comportment of the Muslims in these times has become an evil type of comportment. It is based on treachery. You will find that when a Muslim is entrusted with an item or is put in charge of some organization, that most of the time, he displays nothing but treachery and deceit, contrary to the enemies of Islaam, for they display good conduct for the sake of worldly reasons, not to mention trustworthiness. The following question remains: Does Islaam command us to be treacherous and deceptive? Never, for indeed Allaah says in His Noble Book:

إِنَّ اللّهَ يَأْمُرُكُمْ أَن تُؤدُّواْ الأَمَانَاتِ إِلَى أَهْلِهَا وَإِذَا حَكَمْتُم بَيْنَ النَّاسِ أَن تَحْكُمُواْ بِالْعَدْلِ

"Verily Allaah commands that you should render back the trusts to those to whom they are due, and that when you judge between men, that you judge with justice." [Surah An-Nisaa: 58]

And Allaah says:

إِنَّ اللّهَ يَأْمُرُ بِالْعَدْلِ وَالإِحْسَانِ

"Verily, Allaah commands towards justice and moderateness." [Surah An-Nahl: 90]

And He says:

يَا أَيُّهَا الَّذِينَ آمَنُواْ كُونُواْ قَوَّامِينَ بِالْقِسْطِ شُهَدَاء لِلّهِ وَلَوْ عَلَى أَنفُسِكُمْ أَوِ الْوَالِدَيْنِ وَالأَقْرَبِينَ إِن يَكُنْ غَنِيًّا أَوْ فَقَيرًا فَاللّهُ أَوْلَى بِهِمَا فَلاَ تَتَّبِعُواْ الْهَوَى أَن تَعْدِلُواْ وَإِن تَلْوُواْ أَوْ تُعْرِضُواْ فَإِنَّ اللّهَ كَانَ بِمَا تَعْمَلُونَ خَبِيرًا

"O you who believe! Stand out firmly for justice, as witnesses to Allaah, even though it be against yourselves or your parents or your kin, be he rich or poor. Allaah is a better protector to both than you. So do not

follow your desires, lest you avoid being just. And if you distort your testimony or refuse to give it, then verily, Allaah is All-Aware of what you do." [Surah An-Nisaa: 135]

So it is upon the Muslim to fear Allaah. Many people in Indonesia accepted Islaam as a result of good conduct. This was due to the good conduct and behavior that they saw from the Muslims. For example, a Muslim would go from Hadramaut (in Yemen) to Indonesia for business purposes and they would see his good manners and thus accept Islaam because of that. And yet this man only traveled there for the purpose of conducting business. However, they saw his good manners and dealings and embraced Islaam because of that.

This was the same case with the trustworthiness and honesty of the Companions. They were able to conquer Persia and Rome because of what the people saw from their trustworthiness. But as for us, then whoever desires to learn about Islaam should read about it from books and not learn it from many of those (Muslims) that immigrated to his country. This is since most of those Muslims that immigrated to these foreign (non-Islamic) countries only did so for the sake of worldly reasons and to attain worldly luxuries. So they are prepared to commit the unlawful and prohibited. In fact, some of them even feel ashamed to say they're Muslim while in foreign (non-Islamic) countries!

The Lord of glory and honor says in His Noble Book:

وَمَنْ أَحْسَنُ قَوْلًا مِّمَّن دَعَا إِلَى اللَّهِ وَعَمِلَ صَالِحًا وَقَالَ إِنَّنِي مِنَ الْمُسْلِمِينَ

"And who is better in speech than he who calls to Allaah and does righteous deeds and says: 'I am from the Muslims.'" [Surah Fussilat: 33]

This means that he says: "I am Muslim regardless of whichever country I live in." It is not proper for him to feel ashamed to say that he's Muslim. If only the Muslims would be upright! Several male and female orientalist writers that studied Islamic books said that if only the Muslims were to be upright, America would have embraced Islaam without any struggle or bullets. However, we have gone astray. It is the Muslims that have caused many people to become discouraged from accepting Islaam.

So we advise the brother, may Allaah grant us and him success, to consider himself as fleeing for the sake of his Religion from trials (*fitan*), and to not intend (by his travel) Hijrah. Or he should consider himself - and this is the highest level - as being a Caller to Allaah, for indeed Allaah says in His Noble Book:

وَلْتَكُن مِّنكُمْ أُمَّةٌ يَدْعُونَ إِلَى الْخَيْرِ وَيَأْمُرُونَ بِالْمَعْرُوفِ وَيَنْهَوْنَ عَنِ الْمُنكَرِ وَأُولَـٰئِكَ هُمُ الْمُفْلِحُونَ

"Let there arise out of you a group of people inviting to all that is good, enjoining goodness (i.e. Tawheed) and forbidding evil (i.e. Shirk). And it is they who are the successful." [Surah Aali 'Imraan: 104]

And Allaah says in His Noble Book:

قُلْ هَـٰذِهِ سَبِيلِي أَدْعُو إِلَى اللَّهِ عَلَىٰ بَصِيرَةٍ أَنَا وَمَنِ اتَّبَعَنِي

"Say: This is my way. I call to Allaah upon clear insight (i.e. sure knowledge) - I and those who follow me." [Surah Yoosuf: 108]

This is especially the case since the questions the brother asked lead us to believe that he is a student of knowledge. The people are in need of students of knowledge and they are in need of the conveyance of this Religion, as it was brought to us by the Prophet, and Allaah knows best. [124]

Question: Ibn Qudaamah stated in *al-Mughnee* that people are divided into three categories with regard to Hijrah. **First:** The one who is not able to establish the rites of the Religion while at the same time having the ability to migrate. This type of person is obligated to make Hijrah. **Second:** The one who is able to establish the Religion. This person is not obligated to migrate, rather it is recommended for him.

Answer: As for the first - in fact all of the three are valid - the proof for it is: **"Verily, as for those whom the angels take (in death) while they are wronging themselves (by not performing Hijrah), they (angels) will say**

---

[124] *Ijaabat-us-Saa'il 'alaa Ahamm-il-Masaa'il* (pg. 606-613)

(to them): 'In what (condition) were you?' They will reply: 'We were weak and oppressed in the earth.' They (angels) will say: 'Was not the earth of Allaah spacious enough for you to migrate therein?' Such men will find their abode in Hell - what an evil destination!" [Surah An-Nisaa: 97]

Then He states: **"Except for the weak ones..."** There follows a proof for another group. But as for this first group, then yes, it is considered obligatory for them to migrate. [125]

Question: What about the second group of people that are able to establish their Religion and thus Hijrah is not obligatory on them, but rather (just) recommended. Is this correct?

Answer: This is a correct statement. If one is able to establish the rites of the Religion, then it (i.e. Hijrah) is recommended, unless in the case where he fears afflictions and trials (*fitnah*) befalling him.

Meaning: He is okay when he is in his home and in his masjid, but when he goes out amidst the community he fears that he will be tested by the women who are clothed yet naked. So it is obligatory upon him to migrate if he fears *fitnah* (trials and afflictions) for himself. And if this is not the case, then Hijrah is recommended (on him) as he (i.e. Ibn Qudaamah), may Allaah have mercy on him, stated. [126]

Question: The third category consists of those that are not able to establish the rites of the Religion and at the same time are not able to migrate, so it is not obligatory on him.

Answer: Allaah says after mentioning the ayah of Hijrah, which we just recited before: **"Except the weak ones among men, women and children who cannot devise a plan, nor are they able to find a way. These are the ones whom Allaah is (most) likely to forgive."** [Surah An-Nisaa: 98] [127]

---

[125] *Ar-Rihlatul-Akheerah Li-Imaam-il-Jazeerah* (pg. 158)

[126] *Ar-Rihlatul-Akheerah* (pg. 158-159)

[127] ibid. (pg. 159); **Translator's Note:** These last three questions were presented by Fareed 'Abdullaah to Imaam Muqbil during his stay in Los Angeles prior to his death.

Question: What is the ruling on residing in the Lands of Disbelief, such as America?

Answer: What I believe, may Allaah preserve you, is that residing in this country is not permissible except in the case of a person that fears he will fall into ruin (if he is not there), such as one fleeing from a tyrannical ruler or a sick person that cannot find doctors outside of this country who can treat him. More importantly, I am referring to one who fears destruction for himself (thus causing him to be in America).

While we were in Yemen, we used to hear - and hearing is not like witnessing for it has been authentically reported that the Prophet ﷺ said: **"Hearing news is not like seeing it first-hand"** - we used to hear reports about the women, but it was not as we witnessed with our own eyes.

Therefore, whoever is able to travel to an Islamic country, in spite of the evil that can be found there - especially traveling to Yemen and Saudi Arabia - then there is much good in that. This is especially the case with going to the lands of Najd and to the Haramain (i.e. Makkah and Madeenah), and also other lands such as the villages in Yemen, for all praise be to Allaah you don't hear anything about this or that. But as for here (in America), then it is (just) immorality and demoralization, as you can see.

The Messenger of Allaah ﷺ said: **"I have not left behind a trial after me that is worse for the men than women."** He ﷺ also said: **"I have not seen anyone more deficient in intellect and religion that has the ability to change the mind of a resolute man other than one of you (women)."** And he ﷺ said: **"Verily, the first trial of the Tribe of Israa'eel was with the women, so fear the worldly life and fear women."** And Allaah says:

فَلَا تَخْضَعْنَ بِالْقَوْلِ فَيَطْمَعَ الَّذِي فِي قَلْبِهِ مَرَضٌ

"And do not be soft in speech, lest he in whose is a disease is moved with desire." [Surah Al-Ahzaab: 32]

This (is with regard to that time), so what do you think is the case with what we witnessed from those things that you are more aware of than us. While I was on the plane from this city to that city in which we arrived – I didn't memorize their names – we found such scenes inside the television that by Allaah I wished for death. By my Lord, I wished for death due to the scenes, immorality and demoralization that we saw. Allaah will never neglect you. So how many students of knowledge are patient with three-thousand and four-thousand and five-thousand (Yemeni riyals) and Allaah blesses him in that. And the blessing is from Allaah. And Allaah is the One whom we ask for help. [128]

Question: You mentioned and focused on Hijrah, so some of the brothers have become determined to migrate to Muslim lands. Some of them say: "We will rely on work" while others say: "We will rely on teaching." But in general, many of the brothers and sisters continue to ask about this and would like for you to respond to this issue, may Allaah grant you success.

Answer: I did not focus on Hijrah, even though Hijrah is from the greatest acts of worship. Allaah says: **"Verily, as for those whom the angels take (in death) while they are wronging themselves (by not performing Hijrah), they (angels) will say (to them): 'In what (condition) were you?' They will reply: 'We were weak and oppressed in the earth.' They (angels) will say: 'Was not the earth of Allaah spacious enough for you to migrate therein?' Such men will find their abode in Hell – what an evil destination!"** [Surah An-Nisaa: 97]

And He says: **"And whoever leaves his home as an emigrant unto Allaah and His Messenger, and death overtakes him, his reward is then surely incumbent upon Allaah."** [Surah An-Nisaa: 100]

And the Prophet ﷺ said: **"Hijrah will not cease until repentance ceases. And repentance will not cease (to be accepted) until the sun rises from the place where it sets (i.e. the west)."**

So it is considered as being one of the greatest acts of worship, and it may (at times) be obligatory. However, I was not speaking about Hijrah. I was speaking about fleeing with the Religion for the sake of what? I fear that you will reach the Muslim lands and your remaining there will not be made easy for you. So perhaps you did not make Hijrah your intention. But as for the case where you did make it your intention to make Hijrah, then it is not permissible for you to go back to that country form where you left. This is

[128] *Ar-Rihlatul-Akheerah Li-Imaam-il-Jazeerah* (pg. 189-190)

since the Prophet ﷺ did not permit the Muhaajireen to remain in Makkah after performing Hajj beyond three days. So I had advised you (previously) to flee to Allaah and to leave in order to seek knowledge.

Afterward, if Allaah makes it easy for you to remain in the Lands of Islaam, then that is better. This is since in the Lands of Disbelief, you are at threat with regard to your Religion from the trials of the worldly life and the trials of women. And you are also at threat with being at odds with your family and with the threat of your children being taken away from you. So due to all this, if you are able to flee to Allaah (to a Muslim land), then do it. And Allaah is the One whom we ask for assistance.

We have heard many cases - perhaps you are aware of more cases than we have heard - of a woman going to the police and complaining about her husband and refusing to go back with him, and another case of a woman taking on a lover and so on. So based on all of this, we advise that you should flee to Allaah. I hope you have understood what I intended, may Allaah preserve you. [129]

---

[129] *Ar-Rihlatul-Akheerah Li-Imaam-il-Jazeerah* (pg. 242-243); **Translator's Note:** It is important to note here that the last five questions Imaam Muqbil bin Haadee Al-Waadi'ee answered were during his final journey, which included his travel to the United States, prior to his death. It is clear from reviewing all of these statements collectively that he agreed with the categorical ruling of Hijrah as it applies to people, which was summarized by Imaam Ibn Qudaamah. He further went on to encourage and incite the Muslims in America to leave from that land to go to a Muslims country due to the many dangers present there that he witnessed. When asked for a further clarification on this issue, he stated that he did not intend Hijrah with his speech but rather that the people should flee for the sake of their Religion to the Muslim lands. This is since he was aware of the difficulties and restrictions of Hijrah and due to his view that if a person intends Hijrah when leaving a Land of Disbelief that he could not return back to it. These statements are in conformity with the rest of his statements found in his previous works which have been quoted here, and Allaah knows best.

Appendix H: The Statement of Shaikh Saalih bin Fawzaan bin 'Abdillaah Al-Fawzaan

In his explanation of *Sittah Mawaadi' min as-Seerah* (Six Examples from the Prophet's Biography) of Imaam Muhammad bin 'Abdil-Wahhaab, Shaikh Saalih Al-Fawzaan said:

Hijrah, according to the language, is derived from the word *hajar*, which means to abandon something. Allaah says:

وَالرُّجْزَ فَاهْجُرْ

"And abandon the idols." [Surah Al-Mudaththir: 5] Meaning: "Leave them."

So *hajar* means to abandon something. An example of this is *hajar* of the sinners and *hajar* of the polytheists, meaning to abandon them and not hold love for them. The Prophet ﷺ said: **"The Muhaajir (emigrant) is he who abandons what Allaah has forbidden."** [130]

As for the definition of Hijrah, according to the Religion, then it is to move from a Land of Shirk to a Land of Islaam for the sake of the Religion. This is the religious type of Hijrah. There is a great virtue in Hijrah. It is of the same standing as Faith and Jihaad in the Cause of Allaah.

إِنَّ الَّذِينَ آمَنُوا وَهَاجَرُوا وَجَاهَدُوا بِأَمْوَالِهِمْ وَأَنفُسِهِمْ فِي سَبِيلِ اللَّهِ

"Verily, those who believed and migrated (made Hijrah) and strove hard in Jihaad with their wealth and their lives in the Cause of Allaah" [Surah Al-Anfaal: 72]

This shows the greatness of Hijrah. Hijrah will remain constant until the Final Hour is established. So the one who is not able to openly practice his religion while in the lands of the polytheists is obligated to migrate to a land in which he is able to openly practice it. So if he doesn't migrate even

[130] Reported by Abu Dawood (2481), An-Nasaa'ee in *al-Kubraa* (8701), Ibn Hibbaan (230) and Ahmad (6515)

though he has the ability to do so, he is the one about whom Allaah revealed the following verse: "**Verily, as for those whom the angels take (in death) while they are wronging themselves, they (angels) will say (to them): 'In what were you?' They will reply: 'We were weak and oppressed in the earth.' They (angels) will say: 'Was not the earth of Allaah spacious enough for you to migrate therein?' Such men will find their abode in Hell – what an evil destination!**" [Surah An-Nisaa: 97]

This is a severe threat in spite of the fact that they are Muslims. However, when they failed to make Hijrah due to love of their wealth, children and homeland and gave precedence to love of these things over Hijrah, Allaah warned them with this threat. The reason for the revelation of this *ayah*: During the Battle of Badr, the pagan Arabs were accompanied by some of the Muslims that had remained in Makkah and didn't migrate (to Madeenah) due to their intense love for their homeland, country, property and children even though they had the ability to migrate.

So when the pagan Arabs went out to fight on the Day of *Al-Badr*, these Muslims also went out with them against their choice, since the polytheists had forced them go out with them. Then as the battled ensued, a group of people amongst them were killed while they had been in the ranks of the disbelievers. The Muslims were not aware of who they were (at the time of fighting). But when they realized who they were, they felt sad and said: **"We have killed our brothers."** So Allaah revealed His saying: **"Verily, as for those whom the angels take (in death) while they are wronging themselves, they (angels) will say (to them): 'In what were you?'"**

Meaning: "What is the land that you are in? Which land (is it)?" They did not say: "What is your condition with regard to Faith?" or "How is your certainty?" They will not ask them these things. Rather, they will only ask them about their place **"In what (land) were you?"**

"They (angels) will say (to them): 'In what were you?' They will reply: 'We were weak and oppressed in the earth.'" Meaning: We were forced to go out and fight due to our weakness, and we were not able to refuse.

"They (angels) will say: 'Was not the earth of Allaah spacious enough for you to migrate therein?'" You had a choice in the matter. If you would have migrated like your brothers did, you would have been saved from this incident.

"Such men will find their abode in Hell." This is a threat. **"What an evil destination! Except the weak ones..."** meaning those who do not have the ability to migrate and remain in the lands of Shirk due to their inability to leave.

"Except the weak ones among men, women and children who cannot devise a plan, nor are they able to find a way (to make Hijrah). These are the ones whom Allaah is (most) likely to forgive, and Allaah is Ever Oft-Pardoning, Most Forgiving. And whoever migrates in the Way of Allaah, he will find many dwelling places and plenty (of sustenance) to live by. And whoever leaves his home as an emigrant unto Allaah and His Messenger, and death overtakes him, his reward is then surely incumbent upon Allaah. And Allaah is Ever Oft-Forgiving, Most Merciful." [Surah An-Nisaa: 97-100]

This is with respect to the condition of these people. This is an amazing and profound story - that when these people, in spite of their Islaam and truthfulness to Islaam, abandoned Hijrah for other than a valid reason, this threat befell them as well as this reprimanding of them at the hands of the angels when they came to take their souls (at the time of death). This shows that it is not permissible for a Muslim monotheist to take this matter lightly by remaining with the polytheists, even if he doesn't hold love for them, but rather love for his wealth, children, home and so on.

قُلْ إِن كَانَ آبَاؤُكُمْ وَأَبْنَآؤُكُمْ وَإِخْوَانُكُمْ وَأَزْوَاجُكُمْ وَعَشِيرَتُكُمْ وَأَمْوَالٌ اقْتَرَفْتُمُوهَا وَتِجَارَةٌ تَخْشَوْنَ كَسَادَهَا وَمَسَاكِنُ تَرْضَوْنَهَا أَحَبَّ إِلَيْكُم مِّنَ اللَّهِ وَرَسُولِهِ وَجِهَادٍ فِي سَبِيلِهِ فَتَرَبَّصُوا حَتَّى يَأْتِيَ اللَّهُ بِأَمْرِهِ وَاللَّهُ لاَ يَهْدِي الْقَوْمَ الْفَاسِقِينَ

"Say: If your fathers, your sons, your brothers, your wives, your kindred, the wealth that you have gained, the commerce in which you fear a decline, and the dwellings in which you delight are dearer to you than Allaah and His Messenger, and striving hard and fighting in His Cause, then wait until Allaah brings about His decision (torment). And Allaah guides not the people who are disobedient." [Surah At-Tawbah: 24]

So it is not permissible to place one's love for his property and children over his obedience to Allaah and migrating and fighting in the Cause of Allaah. Many people read these verses but yet do not reflect on them.

The Companions only called them **"our brothers"** because they still were upon their religion. They did not state that they sided with the polytheists or that they praised the polytheists. Rather, those individuals hated the religion of the polytheists and were upon Tawheed, sincerely worshipping Allaah and not having any hypocrisy. But they left off doing one thing, which was Hijrah, without a valid reason. So Allaah blamed them for that.

This is why the angels will not ask them about their faith and beliefs, since they already know that they were upon the correct creed and possessed true faith. Rather, they will ask them about the place that they were in, since it is not permissible for them to stay there when they are able to migrate from it.

The angels did not say (in the ayah): "You have lied. You are not Muslims. You are not believers." Rather, they said: **"In what were you."** So they asked them about the place in which they were presently living, which was the cause for them going out to fight alongside the polytheists, even if they were forced to do it. This is since they were the cause for the disbelievers taking over them. It is not permissible to accompany them and go out with them out of love for one's property and family. [131]

---

[131] Refer to his explanation of *Sittah Mawaadi' min as-Seerah* (pg. 45-51) published by *Dar al-Kitab wa Sunnah*, Algeria, 2005.

Appendix I: The Statement of Shaikh 'Ubayd bin 'Abdillaah bin Sulaymaan Al-Jaabiree

In his explanation of *Thalaathat-ul-Usool,* Shaikh 'Ubayd Al-Jaabiree, said:

The author states: "Hijrah means: Moving from a Land of Shirk to a Land of Islaam. It is obligatory upon this ummah to migrate from a Land of Shirk to a Land of Islaam."

Linguistically, Hijrah means to abandon something. According to custom, it means to move from one land to another. As for the definition of the term Hijrah in the Religion, then it is as the author has stated.

It is an obligation that is well established and not abrogated. A Muslim is obligated to make Hijrah if he lives in one of the lands of the disbelievers and has no security as regards to his religion and honor. But in the case where he does feel secure as regards to his religion and honor, it is not binding upon him to make Hijrah, rather it is just recommended. Regardless, it is better to migrate from the lands of the disbelievers to the lands of Islaam. The proofs for the establishment of the ruling on Hijrah are clear and authentic from the Sunnah and the Noble Qur'aan.

The author continues: "And it is everlasting until the (Final) Hour is established. The proof for this is Allaah's saying: **'Verily, as for those whom the angels take (in death) while they are wronging themselves (by not performing Hijrah), they (angels) will say (to them): 'In what (condition) were you?' They will reply: 'We were weak and oppressed in the earth.' They (angels) will say: 'Was not the earth of Allaah spacious enough for you to migrate therein?' Such men will find their abode in Hell - what an evil destination! Except the weak ones among men, women and children - who cannot devise a plan, nor are they able to direct their way. These are the ones whom Allaah is (most) likely to forgive, and Allaah is Ever Oft-Pardoning, Most Forgiving.'** [Surah An-Nisaa: 97-99]"

This *ayah* clearly shows that Hijrah will remain. The basis of proof in this *ayah* is found in the angels' reprimanding of those who are satisfied with being debased and oppressed in their Religion and not migrating even though they have the ability to do it. This is why Allaah says after that:

"Except the weak ones." If a person is afflicted with regard to his religion at the hands of the disbelievers and is not able to make Hijrah, he bears no sin. But in the case where he chooses to remain and surrenders his religion and honor even though he has the ability to leave, this is the person that is subject to the threat, as is evident in the context of the verse.

The author continues: "Allaah says: **'O My servants who believe (in Me)! Verily, My earth is spacious so to Me alone, perform your worship.'** [Surah Al-'Ankaboot: 56]"

This means: If they are not able to worship Allaah in a Land of Disbelief, it is required upon them to migrate to either a Muslim land or a non-Muslim land in which they have the ability to worship Allaah in the correct manner.

The author said: "Al-Baghawee, may Allaah have mercy on him, said: 'The reason for the revelation of this *ayah* was due to some Muslims who had resided in Makkah and did not migrate (to Madeenah). Allaah called out to them using the title of Eemaan (for them).'"

As has been agreed upon the scholars that derive principles, consideration is given to the generality of the wording and not to the specificity of the cause. So if there occurs a general wording with respect to a specific issue, this means that the text remains in its general sense with that specific issue, for which reason the text was revealed, falling under that generality first and foremost.

The author, may Allaah have mercy on him, said: "The proof for Hijrah from the Sunnah is his ﷺ saying: **'Hijrah will not cease until repentance ceases (to be accepted). And repentance will not cease (to be accepted) until the sun rises from where it sets (i.e. the west).'"**

This hadeeth indicates two things, and they are:

1. That Hijrah is well-established and firmly-rooted, and that its termination will only occur when repentance terminates.

2. It shows that repentance has a limit – this is its universal time-frame, and that is when the sun rises from the west. [132]

---

[132] *Ittihaaf-ul-'Uqool bi-Sharh ath-Thalaathat-il-Usool* (pg. 136-140)

Appendix J: The Statement of Shaikh Ahmad bin Yahyaa bin Muhammad An-Najmee

In his explanation of *Thalaathat-ul-Usool* of Imaam Muhammad bin 'Abdil-Wahhaab, Shaikh Ahmad An-Najmee said:

The definition of Hijrah is: To abandon the Land of Shirk, i.e. to leave it, and to come to a Land of Islaam. This is since the word Hijrah is derived from the root *hajr* which means to abandon or leave off. The Muslims were commanded to abandon the Land of Shirk and go to the Land of Islaam. The ruling on Hijrah is that it is obligatory for the one who is able to do it. This is why Allaah informs us that there will be a group of people whom the angels will take in death while they are wronging themselves due to their lack of migrating and their preferring the Land of Shirk. Allaah says:

إِنَّ الَّذِينَ تَوَفَّاهُمُ الْمَلاَئِكَةُ ظَالِمِي أَنْفُسِهِمْ قَالُوا فِيمَ كُنتُمْ قَالُوا كُنَّا مُسْتَضْعَفِينَ فِي الأَرْضِ قَالُوَا أَلَمْ تَكُنْ أَرْضُ اللهِ وَاسِعَةً فَتُهَاجِرُوا فِيهَا فَأُوْلَـئِكَ مَأْوَاهُمْ جَهَنَّمُ وَسَاءتْ مَصِيرًا . إِلاَّ الْمُسْتَضْعَفِينَ مِنَ الرِّجَالِ وَالنِّسَاء وَالْوِلْدَانِ لاَ يَسْتَطِيعُونَ حِيلَةً وَلاَ يَهْتَدُونَ سَبِيلاً . فَأُوْلَـئِكَ عَسَى اللهُ أَن يَعْفُوَ عَنْهُمْ وَكَانَ اللهُ عَفُوًّا غَفُورًا

"Verily, as for those whom the angels take (in death) while they are wronging themselves (by not performing Hijrah), they (angels) will say (to them): 'In what (condition) were you?' They will reply: 'We were weak and oppressed in the earth.' They (angels) will say: 'Was not the earth of Allaah spacious enough for you to migrate therein?' Such men will find their abode in Hell - what an evil destination! Except the weak ones among men, women and children - who cannot devise a plan, nor are they able to direct their way. These are the ones whom Allaah is (most) likely to forgive, and Allaah is Ever Oft-Pardoning, Most Forgiving." [Surah An-Nisaa: 97-99] And He says:

يَا عِبَادِيَ الَّذِينَ آمَنُوا إِنَّ أَرْضِي وَاسِعَةٌ فَإِيَّايَ فَاعْبُدُون

"O My servants who believe (in Me)! Verily, My earth is spacious so to Me alone, perform your worship." [Surah Al-'Ankaboot: 56]

Al-Baghawee, may Allaah have mercy on him, said: "The reason for the revelation of this *ayah* was due to some Muslims who had resided in Makkah and did not migrate (to Madeenah). Allaah called out to them using the title of Eemaan (for them)."

We derive from these verses that Hijrah is obligatory on the one who is able to do it, which requires him to move from a Land of Disbelief to a Land of Islaam. This is since in a Land of Disbelief, the believer is exposed to harm and the government will be against him as opposed to in his favor. Even though he may be safe from harm, he will still not be safe from having to seek judgement in laws that are not from Allaah's Legislation, such as man-made laws, which they use to govern the people.

However, Hijrah in our present time must only be done with the permission from the country that one is migrating to. So if the country refuses to accept this emigrant, then he has no ability or power in the matter except by Allaah's leave.

Things used to be easy (in the old days). But as for today, there is difficulty in Hijrah either from the side of the country that one is migrating from or from the side of the country that one is migrating to. So whoever is able to make Hijrah, with ease and no difficulty, to a Land of Islaam, then such a person is obligated to do that. Furthermore, some of the Muslim countries today apply strict measures against those who adhere to the Religion of Allaah in everything that he brings and leaves behind.

In summary, any Muslim that lives in a country, which the disbelievers rule based on man-made laws, must migrate from it if he is easily able to do it. And if it is not easy for him, then according to what is apparent (from the texts), he is excused due to Allaah's saying:

لا يُكَلِّفُ اللهُ نَفْسًا إِلاَّ وُسْعَهَا

"Allaah does not burden a soul with more than it can handle." [Surah Al-Baqarah: 286]. And with Allaah lies the success. [133]

[133] See his commentary (*ta'leeqaat*) notes to *Thalaathat-ul-Usool* (pg. 53-54)

Appendix K: The Statement of Shaikh Zayd bin Muhammad bin Haadee Al-Madkhalee

In his explanation of *Thalaathat-ul-Usool*, Shaikh Zayd bin Muhammad Al-Madkhalee said:

After completing a period of thirteen years (in Makkah), the Prophet was ordered to make Hijrah. So he migrated to Madeenah. Prior to this, a delegation from Madeenah had come to him, so he gathered them at 'Aqabah during the Hajj season and taught them the rites of Islaam. They believed in him, confirmed his Message and returned to their families spreading the Call of Islaam and awaiting the arrival of the Prophet ﷺ. And he came to them after some time had passed. Hijrah served as one of the greatest doors to good that was opened for the world, since with it the amount of Companions of the Prophet grew in number, the Call spread and the verses on Jihaad were revealed against those who stood as barriers against the Call and those who prevented people from the Right Path.

Allaah commanded His Prophet ﷺ and those with him to fight against them. So decisions were made, armies were gathered, and ensuing battles took place. Victory was sworn to them. Even though they faced defeat at times, they bore it with patience and tolerance, and that did not turn them back from continuing on the path of Jihaad and Calling to Islaam.

So Hijrah became one of the obligations that Allaah made binding upon whoever accepted Islaam while living in the Lands of Disbelief. In fact, He condemned those who stayed amongst the disbelievers where they were not able to openly practice the rites of Islaam. Allaah condemned them because of their devotion to their homelands and properties, where He said:

إِنَّ الَّذِينَ تَوَفَّاهُمُ الْمَلآئِكَةُ ظَالِمِي أَنْفُسِهِمْ قَالُوا فِيمَ كُنتُمْ قَالُوا كُنَّا مُسْتَضْعَفِينَ فِي الأَرْضِ قَالْوَاْ أَلَمْ تَكُنْ أَرْضُ اللّهِ وَاسِعَةً فَتُهَاجِرُواْ فِيهَا فَأُوْلَـئِكَ مَأْوَاهُمْ جَهَنَّمُ وَسَاءتْ مَصِيرًا . إِلاَّ الْمُسْتَضْعَفِينَ مِنَ الرِّجَالِ وَالنِّسَاء وَالْوِلْدَانِ لاَ يَسْتَطِيعُونَ حِيلَةً وَلاَ يَهْتَدُونَ سَبِيلاً . فَأُوْلَـئِكَ عَسَى اللّهُ أَن يَعْفُوَ عَنْهُمْ وَكَانَ اللّهُ عَفُوًّا غَفُورًا

"Verily, as for those whom the angels take (in death) while they are wronging themselves (by not performing Hijrah), they (angels) will say (to them): 'In what (condition) were you?' They will reply: 'We were weak and oppressed in the earth.' They (angels) will say: 'Was not the earth of Allaah spacious enough for you to migrate therein?' Such men will find their abode in Hell - what an evil destination! Except the weak ones among men, women and children - who cannot devise a plan, nor are they able to direct their way. These are the ones whom Allaah is (most) likely to forgive, and Allaah is Ever Oft-Pardoning, Most Forgiving." [Surah An-Nisaa: 97-99]

So these are a people that Allaah excused for not being able to perform Hijrah, either because they feared for their lives from the backlash of the leaders of disbelief or because they had no ability that enabled them to get to Madeenah.

The ruling on Hijrah from the Lands of Disbelief to the Lands of Islaam continued to remain established until the Day of Judgement. The Lands of Disbelief are those countries in which other than Allaah is worshipped and which are governed by other than His Laws. It is also the land in which a Muslim is not able to establish the rites of Islaam.

The Lands of Islaam are those lands that are governed according to Allaah's Laws and in which the rites of the Religion are established, at the head of which is singling out the Lord of all that exists for worship and suppressing polytheism and the polytheists. Even though sins and individual disbelievers can be found there, it is still considered a Land of Islaam. As long as the rule there is in accordance with Allaah's Laws, the land is purified from false gods, the banner of Tawheed (Allaah's Oneness) is raised high, the rites of Islaam are established, and the sacred Houses of Allaah are built there, then it is a Land of Islaam, regardless of what condition it is in.

So whoever lives in a Land of Disbelief, whilst being a Muslim, is obligated to migrate to a Land of Islaam, unless he falls under one of those whom Allaah excused - i.e. such as the weak (men), women, or children. Since these individuals are not able to perform Hijrah, Allaah has excused them and promised to forgive them. As for those who are able to migrate but nothing holds them back except for materialistic reasons such as money, children and love for one's birthplace, then such people are defeated, i.e. the proofs are against them. They have oppressed themselves and should not expect anything less than what Allaah stated when He said:

إِنَّ الَّذِينَ تَوَفَّاهُمُ الْمَلاَئِكَةُ ظَالِمِي أَنْفُسِهِمْ قَالُوا فِيمَ كُنْتُمْ

"Verily, as for those whom the angels take (in death) while they are wronging themselves (by not performing Hijrah), they (angels) will say (to them): 'In what (condition) were you?'..." [Surah An-Nisaa: 97]

The angels, by Allaah's command, will rebuke this group of people that had the ability to leave from the Land of Disbelief, but didn't.

There are some issues related to this discussion, which are:

The prohibition of traveling to the lands of the People of Disbelief without any compelling need to do so, and choosing freely to reside in those lands.

Adding further evil to this is when a person prefers the Lands of Disbelief, while at the same time he criticizes the Lands of Islaam. This is the most ignorant of people and the farthest of mankind in awareness of the truth. It is as if this person is blind and the path of guidance has not been clarified to him from the paths of falsehood.

Therefore, fleeing from a land is only to be done from the Lands of Disbelief to the Lands of Islaam, whatever their condition may be. This is since the Prophet ﷺ warned us about intermingling with the polytheists, relying upon them for support, and living with them, unless one is compelled to do so by some emergency situation.

As for the one who goes there to call the people to Islaam, whilst being fortified with knowledge of the Religion and equipped with the means that will prevent him from falling into detestable acts or deviating in the people's concepts, then such a person is like a warrior that goes out to fight against them through the means of calling to good, then returns back to his homeland. This is especially the case if there is an Islamic country that is organizing these operations.

There may be some emergency situation that compels one to go to a Land of Disbelief, such as going for medical treatment, or to learn some science that the Muslim ummah needs and which cannot be found in their lands, or to represent a Muslim country in some required national service.

These are situations in which a Muslim is exempted. However, no one should go except for someone who is fortified with religious knowledge, Taqwaa, Faith, and fear of Allaah. As for a reason other than this, then the souls will not find tranquility except in the lands and countries of Islaam. A person should protect his life, religion, wealth and blood, and he should worship Allaah while being pleased with that and not fearing any of the causes of deviation or transgression or ridiculing of his Religion, which the disbelievers do with the followers of Islaam, for the most part, if they are able to.

The proof that the ruling on Hijrah is continuous and remains in effect is Allaah's statement:

يَا عِبَادِيَ الَّذِينَ آمَنُوا إِنَّ أَرْضِي وَاسِعَةٌ فَإِيَّايَ فَاعْبُدُونِ

"O My servants who believe (in Me)! Verily, My earth is spacious so to Me alone, perform your worship." [Surah Al-'Ankaboot: 56]

This means: The earth is vast, so one must move from a place of restrictedness to a place of vastness. The lands of restrictedness refer to the Lands of Disbelief, while the lands of vastness refer to the Lands of Islaam.

The Prophet's ﷺ statement: "**Hijrah will not cease until repentance ceases, and repentance will not cease (to be accepted) until the sun rises from where it sets (i.e. the west)**'[134] is proof for its continuity and permanence, as long as its causes are present and its preventing factors are absent.

However, those Muslims that remain in the Lands of Disbelief without a valid religious excuse should not be ruled as being disbelievers. Rather, they have fallen into one of the major sins. This is unless they fall into one of the causes that takes them from their (present) Islaam to disbelief, and

---

[134] Reported by Abu Dawood in his *Sunan*: Book of Jihaad 3/3 (2479) and Ahmad (1/192 & 4/99). The hadeeth is authentic. See *Irwaa-ul-Ghaleel* (5/33, no. 1208)

we seek refuge in Allaah from that! An example of this is such as if they prefer living with the disbelievers over living with Islaam and the Muslims or if they feel that their pure and blessed happiness and livelihood can only be achieved in the Lands of Disbelief and that a life of hardship and misfortune lies in the Lands of Islaam. This, and we seek refuge in Allaah, is remoteness from Allaah, severe deviation, and a great calamity. The cause behind all of this is ignorance of Islaam. [135]

---

[135] An excerpt from his explanation of *Thalaathat-ul-Usool* called: *Tareeq-ul-Wusool ilaa Eedaah ath-Thalaathat-il-Usool* (pg. 210-215) with slight abridgement.

Appendix L: The Statement of Shaikh Saalih bin 'Abdil-'Azeez Aali Shaikh

In his explanation of the *Thalaathat-ul-Usool*, Shaikh Saalih Aali Shaikh said:

The author (i.e. Ibn 'Abdil-Wahhaab) has interpreted Hijrah as: "Moving from a Land of Shirk to a Land of Islaam." This is its terminology definition. Linguistically, it means to abandon something. And according to its religious definition, it means to abandon that which Allaah doesn't love and is not pleased with. What falls under this religious definition is the rejection of polytheism. It also entails abandoning what Allaah and His Messenger hate and abandoning the Lands of Disbelief since Allaah is not pleased with that nor does He love that His servants reside in such lands.

As for the meaning of its term, the author states that it means: "Moving from a Land of Shirk to a Land of Islaam."

"Moving" means: Abandoning a Land of Shirk and going to a Land of Islaam. The reason for Hijrah, i.e. the reason for the obligation of Hijrah or the reason for its legislation, is due to the fact that the believer is obligated to openly manifest his Religion, feel proud of it, and clarify it to the people, informing them that he bears witness to the testimony of truth. This is since bearing witness that Allaah is the only one true God and that His Prophet is His Messenger entails informing others. And this informing can be by way of statements and actions and outwardly manifesting the Religion with it.

This is why migrating from a Land of Shirk to a Land of Islaam is obligatory if a Muslim is not able to openly practice his Religion. Open adherence to the Religion is obligatory on earth. It is incumbent upon a Muslim to openly manifest his Religion and not conceal it. So if it is not possible for him to openly manifest his Religion in a certain country, he is obligated to leave it, i.e. he is obligated to make Hijrah from it.

The author states: "Moving from a Land of Shirk to a Land of Islaam." The Land of Shirk is every Land in which Shirk (polytheism) appears predominantly. If Shirk (polytheism) appears in a country and it becomes dominant and prevalent, more than anything else, it then takes on the name of a "Land of Shirk." This is regardless if the Shirk is with regard to

Allaah's Lordship, the Worship to Him or the requisites of His Worship, such as Obedience (to Him), Ruling by His Laws and so on.

A Land of Shirk is a Land in which polytheism appears and is dominant. This is the definition given by Shaikh Muhammad bin Ibraaheem, may Allaah have mercy on him, when he was asked which land was a Land of Disbelief.

He replied saying: "The Land of Disbelief is the land in which disbelief appears and is predominant and prevalent." So therefore, if Shirk appears in a country and its presence becomes prevalent, meaning that it has spread out and become manifest, clear and foremost, then this country is to be called a "Land of Shirk." This is with regard to what has occurred in it, and that is Shirk. As for with regards to the inhabitants of that country, then this is an issue that the scholars have differed on, which is: One must look at the inhabitants of a country in order to determine whether it is a Land of Islaam or a Land of Shirk.

Shaikh-ul-Islaam Ibn Taimiyyah, may Allaah have mercy on him, was asked about a land in which both the laws of disbelief and the laws of Islaam were established, so he replied that it is not possible to rule that such a country is a Land of Disbelief or a Land of Islaam. Rather, a Muslim should be dealt with according to his beliefs and a disbeliever should be dealt with according to his beliefs. Some scholars held that a country in which the *Adhaan* is manifest and heard during the times of prayer is a Land of Islaam.

The reason for this is that whenever the Prophet ﷺ wanted to attack a people in the morning time, he would tell those with him: **"Wait. If you hear the *Adhaan*, then refrain (from fighting). And if you don't hear any *Adhaan*, then fight."**

However, there is speculation on this since the hadeeth is to be taken in its original sense. And that is that (in the old days) when they would say the *Adhaan* out loud, this meant that they would confirm and bear witness to the testimony of truth since they knew the meaning of that. And they would apply the requisites of Tawheed that are contained in the *Adhaan*. So when they bear witness that there is no deity that has the right to be worshipped except Allaah, and they raise out loud the call to prayer, this means that they have left off Shirk, absolved themselves from it and established the prayer. Allaah says:

فَإِن تَابُوا وَأَقَامُوا الصَّلاَةَ وَآتَوُا الزَّكَاةَ فَإِخْوَانُكُمْ فِي الدِّينِ

"But if they repent and establish the prayer and give the Zakaat, then they are your brothers in the Religion." [Surah At-Tawbah: 11]

This is since the Arabs understood Tawheed. So when they would embrace Islaam and bear witness that there was no deity that had the right to be worshipped except Allaah and that Muhammad was the Messenger of Allaah ﷺ, this meant that they would act upon its requisites. But as for these later times, many Muslims say *"Laa Ilaaha illaa Allaah, Muhammadu Rasoolullaah"* but don't know what it means, nor do they act upon its requisites. Rather, you will find Shirk (polytheism) widespread amongst them. So based on this, we hold that this condition or this definition - which is that a Land of Islaam is a land in which the Call to Prayer is outwardly apparent - is not correct in these current times.

The proof used for it should be based on its original sense, which is that the Arabs would abandon Shirk and free themselves from it and its people, and they would accept Tawheed and act upon the requisites of the two testimonies of Faith, contrary to the people of these current times. The first definition for classifying a land is more correct. And the aspect of judging that a country is either a Land of Shirk or a Land of Islaam is not dependent upon the people that live within the country. Rather, we say: Judging a country to be a Land of Shirk depends on the prevalence of the presence of polytheism and disbelief. And everyone that lives in that country should be treated according to his own self, especially in these times, since the appearance of disbelief and polytheism in many lands did not come about due to the free choice of the inhabitants of those countries. Rather, it may occur as a result of subjugation - either from the Sufi orders, for example, or from the influence of the governments and so on, as is evident and known. Based on this, we say that defining a country depends on what I have just explained, and as for that country's inhabitants, then they vary.

The author states: "Hijrah means: Moving from a Land of Shirk to a Land of Islaam." Hijrah, with respect to its area, is divided into the general Hijrah and the specific Hijrah. The general Hijrah is that which the Shaikh

(Muhammad bin 'Abdil-Wahhaab) defined here, and that is: Leaving a Land of Shirk to go to a Land of Islaam. Moving from the Lands of Shirk to the Lands of Islaam will remain in effect until the sun rises from its place of setting (i.e. west). Any country in which Shirk and the laws of Shirk are apparent, and it is the dominant factor, then migrating from it can be called Hijrah. This Hijrah is general with respect to the area, i.e. it is possible that it can be applied to any country.

As for the specific Hijrah, then it refers to only the Hijrah (migration) from Makkah to Madeenah. When the Prophet ﷺ left Makkah it was still a Land of Shirk. He ﷺ went to Madeenah since Islaam had spread throughout it to the point that it had entered into every household in Madeenah. So it had become a Land of Islaam. When the Prophet ﷺ moved from the Land of Shirk to the Land of Islaam, he made a specific Hijrah. It is this specific Hijrah that the Prophet ﷺ spoke of when he said: **"There is no (more) Hijrah after the Conquest, but rather Jihaad and (good) intention"** as is reported in the *Saheeh* Collection.

The Prophet's ﷺ statement: **"There is no (more) Hijrah after the Conquest"** refers to the Hijrah from Makkah. Therefore, the specific Hijrah was from Makkah to Madeenah. As for the general Hijrah, which is moving from a Land of Shirk to a Land of Islaam, then this remains in effect until the sun rises from its place of setting (i.e. the west) - i.e. when the Final Hour is established so long as there exists a Land of Shirk and a Land of Islaam, Hijrah is binding. This is with regard to the area. As for its ruling, then Hijrah could at times be obligatory and at times be recommended. Hijrah, i.e. from a Land of Shirk to a Land of Islaam, may be obligatory if a Muslim that resides in a Land of Shirk is not able to openly practice his Religion. If he is not able to openly manifest the requisites of his Religion, prayer and following the Sunnah - every country according to how much polytheism lies in it - if he is not able to do that, then Hijrah becomes obligatory upon him. This is how the following statement of Allaah should be interpreted:

إِنَّ الَّذِينَ تَوَفَّاهُمُ الْمَلَآئِكَةُ ظَالِمِي أَنْفُسِهِمْ قَالُوا فِيمَ كُنتُمْ قَالُوا كُنَّا مُسْتَضْعَفِينَ فِي الأَرْضِ

"Verily, as for those whom the angels take (in death) while they are wronging themselves, they (angels) will say (to them): 'In what (condition) were you?' They will reply: 'We were weak and oppressed in the earth.'" [Surah An-Nisaa: 97]

Meaning: We were not able to openly practice our Religion. The weakness here refers to the lack of being able to openly practice one's Religion. **"They (angels) will say: 'Was not the earth of Allaah spacious enough for you to migrate therein?' Such men will find their abode in Hell - what an evil destination!"** [Surah An-Nisaa: 97]

This shows that Hijrah is obligatory, since Allaah has threatened them with Hellfire. So it is forbidden to abandon Hijrah for the one who is not able to openly practice his Religion.

The Second Type: Recommended: Migrating from a Land of Shirk to a Land of Islaam can also be recommended, and that is when the believer who lives in the Land of Shirk is able to openly practice his Religion. This is since the fundamental foundation of Hijrah is that the believer is able to openly practice his Religion and worship Allaah with pride and self-esteem, as Allaah says:

يَا عِبَادِيَ الَّذِينَ آمَنُوا إِنَّ أَرْضِي وَاسِعَةٌ فَإِيَّايَ فَاعْبُدُون

"O My servants who believe (in Me)! Verily, My earth is spacious so to Me alone, perform your worship." [Surah Al-'Ankaboot: 56]

This verse was revealed concerning those who abandoned Hijrah, however Allaah still called them using the title of Eemaan. These rulings apply to migrating from a Land of Disbelief and Shirk to a Land of Islaam. There is also another type of Hijrah, which is from a land in which there are many sins and innovations to a land in which there are no sins and innovations or less sins and innovations.

The scholars of the Hanbalee Fiqh, may Allaah have mercy on them, mentioned that this type of Hijrah is recommended. If a country is filled with major sins and disobedience, it is recommended for him to abandon it and go to a country in which there is less than that or none of that at all. This is since his remaining in that condition with those types of people will cause him to live amongst those who are threatened with the type of punishment that will befall those who wrong themselves (by not making Hijrah).

When the voice of the Mu'tazilah and the voice of the people of innovation became raised high and when sins, fornication and the consumption of alcohol increased, all the people of knowledge made Hijrah from Baghdad, leaving that land to go to another land. Some scholars stayed behind, but they implemented Allaah's rights by establishing the Call to Allaah, clarifying knowledge, forbidding evil and so on. Also, many scholars moved from Egypt when the 'Ubaydee Dynasty took over, leaving it to go somewhere else. This action on their part can be interpreted as being either the recommended form of Hijrah or the obligatory form, in accordance with the conditions of their time.

The author quotes the following *ayah* as proof: **"Verily, as for those whom the angels take (in death) while they are wronging themselves."** They have wronged themselves by not performing Hijrah. This is since they have disobeyed Allaah by not making Hijrah. The believers were not able to openly practice their Religion in Makkah, since the disbelievers had control over its inhabitants. Therefore, the believers weren't able to openly manifest their Religion. This was going on since the beginning of the Call. But they prevailed for a period of time even though openly professing the Religion at the beginning of the Call was not obligatory. Later, they were commanded to do that by Allaah's statement:

فَاصْدَعْ بِمَا تُؤْمَرُ وَأَعْرِضْ عَنِ الْمُشْرِكِينَ . إِنَّا كَفَيْنَـكَ الْمُسْتَهْزِءِينَ

"So openly proclaim what you have been commanded and turn away from the polytheists. Verily, We will suffice you against the mockers." [Surah Al-Hijr: 94-95]

So some of the believers were tested and afflicted and they were not able to openly proclaim their Religion. Because of this, they sought the Prophet's permission to migrate to Abyssinia. He granted them permission to migrate to Abyssinia a first time and then a second time. It is also held that there was a third Hijrah (i.e. migration to Abyssinia). Since it was not possible to openly proclaim and practice the Religion while in Makkah, and a Land of

Islaam had been established in Madeenah, Hijrah became an individual obligation upon each and every Muslim. This is why Allaah says here: **"They (angels) will say (to them)..."** meaning: The angels will speak to those people who died while not having performed Hijrah, saying to them: **"In what (condition) were you?"** This means: "In what state of being were you?" **"They will reply: 'We were weak and oppressed in the earth.'"** So the angels will respond: **"Was not the earth of Allaah spacious enough for you to migrate therein?"** This is a criticism against them, since the interrogatory marker used here: "Was not" is in a critical mode. The rule is that everything that is stated after this interrogatory marker must be false. So if the *hamzah* (interrogative marker) is left out, and the sentence that follows it were to be read (in Arabic) without it, and it reads as a statement that is not correct, this means that the *hamzah* (interrogative marker) was placed there to indicate criticism.

So if the interrogative marker were to be left out, the sentence would read: "Allaah's earth was not spacious enough." Is this correct? It is not correct, since Allaah's earth is spacious. So whenever there occurs a question with the interrogative marker of *hamzah* followed by a sentence, which would be false in the absence of the *hamzah,* this shows that the *hamzah* was placed there in order to denote criticism. This has been explained in the books that clarify the Arabic language.

The *ayah* continues: "...**for you to migrate therein?"** This shows that they left off making Hijrah. This *ayah* has been interpreted (by some) to mean: Whoever doesn't make Hijrah while having the ability to do so that he is a polytheist and disbeliever who is upon the religion of those whom he resides with. This is not correct. Rather, the *ayah* was revealed regarding the believers, since Allaah says in the beginning of it: **"Verily, as for those whom the angels take (in death) while they are wronging themselves."** These people oppressed themselves, but it does not mean the major oppression. Rather, it means the minor form of oppression, by not migrating.

Allaah says after that: **"Except the weak ones among men, women and children - who cannot devise a plan, nor are they able to direct their way."** [Surah An-Nisaa: 98] The weak men are those who are unable to find a way out. They are not able to direct their way to another country. They are not able to devise a plan. They do not have a mode of transport nor do they have money that can transfer them. So they are weak and incapable. The have the desire to make Hijrah, but they are weak from the perspective of not being able to migrate due to a lack of money, mode of transport, guide and so on. Allaah says about these people: **"These are the ones whom Allaah is (most) likely to forgive, and Allaah is Ever Oft-Pardoning, Most Forgiving."** [Surah An-Nisaa: 99]

What also falls under this are those who are not able to make Hijrah in these current times due to present obstacles such as not being granted a visa and its likes. These kinds of people are not able to devise a plan. They yearn to leave the Land of Shirk to go to the Land of Islaam, but they are not able to do it due to the presence of obstacles.

Then the author lists another proof, which is: "And Allaah says: **'O My servants who believe (in Me)! Verily, My earth is spacious so to Me alone, perform your worship.'** [Surah Al-'Ankaboot: 56] Al-Baghawee, may Allaah have mercy on him, said: 'The reason for the revelation of this *ayah* was due to some Muslims who had resided in Makkah and did not migrate (to Madeenah). Allaah called out to them using the title of Eemaan (for them)."

They did not make Hijrah, but yet Allaah still called out to them with the title of Eemaan. This proves that abandoning Hijrah does not strip one of Eemaan (Faith). This means that abandoning Hijrah is neither Major Shirk nor is it Major Disbelief. Rather it is just one of the major sins. This is since Allaah called out to those who didn't make Hijrah using the term Eemaan.

Al-Baghawee's statement shows that not migrating from Makkah does not constitute disbelief or polytheism, and that Allaah's statement in the previous *ayah*: **"Such men will find their abode in Hell - what an evil destination"** is due to the fact that they abandoned one of the obligations and instead committed one of the major sins. However, in spite of this, Eemaan was not removed from them because of their lack of performing Hijrah from the Land of Disbelief to the Land of Islaam. [136]

---

[136] Refer to *Jaami' Shurooh al-Usool-uth-Thalaathah* (pg. 764-771)

Appendix M: The Statement of Shaikh Saalih bin Sa'ad As-Suhaymee

In his explanation of *Thalaathat-ul-Usool*, Shaikh Saalih As-Suhaymee stated the following:

The author mentions some of the rules of Hijrah, stating that it is obligatory. Hijrah means: Moving from a Land of Shirk to a Land of Islaam. So if a Muslim is able to move from a Land of Shirk to a Land of Islaam, then this is obligatory upon him so that he may be able to perform his worship in the most perfect of manners.

In the verses mentioned by the author, Allaah has threatened those who don't migrate even though they have the ability to do it:

إِنَّ الَّذِينَ تَوَفَّاهُمُ الْمَلآئِكَةُ ظَالِمِي أَنْفُسِهِمْ قَالُوا فِيمَ كُنتُمْ قَالُوا كُنَّا مُسْتَضْعَفِينَ فِي الأَرْضِ قَالْوَاْ أَلَمْ تَكُنْ أَرْضُ اللّهِ وَاسِعَةً فَتُهَاجِرُوا فِيهَا فَأُوْلَـئِكَ مَأْوَاهُمْ جَهَنَّمُ وَسَاءتْ مَصِيرًا . إِلاَّ الْمُسْتَضْعَفِينَ مِنَ الرِّجَالِ وَالنِّسَاء وَالْوِلْدَانِ لاَ يَسْتَطِيعُونَ حِيلَةً وَلاَ يَهْتَدُونَ سَبِيلاً . فَأُوْلَـئِكَ عَسَى اللّهُ أَن يَعْفُوَ عَنْهُمْ وَكَانَ اللّهُ عَفُوًّا غَفُورًا

"Verily, as for those whom the angels take (in death) while they are wronging themselves (by not performing Hijrah), they (angels) will say (to them): 'In what (condition) were you?' They will reply: 'We were weak and oppressed in the earth.' They (angels) will say: 'Was not the earth of Allaah spacious enough for you to migrate therein?' Such men will find their abode in Hell - what an evil destination! Except the weak ones among men, women and children - who cannot devise a plan, nor are they able to direct their way. These are the ones whom Allaah is (most) likely to forgive, and Allaah is Ever Oft-Pardoning, Most Forgiving." [Surah An-Nisaa: 97-99]

Allaah then says after this:

وَمَن يُهَاجِرْ فِي سَبِيلِ اللّهِ يَجِدْ فِي الأَرْضِ مُرَاغَمًا كَثِيرًا وَسَعَةً وَمَن يَخْرُجْ مِن بَيْتِهِ مُهَاجِرًا إِلَى اللّهِ وَرَسُولِهِ ثُمَّ يُدْرِكْهُ الْمَوْتُ فَقَدْ وَقَعَ أَجْرُهُ عَلى اللّهِ وَكَانَ اللّهُ غَفُورًا رَّحِيمًا

"And whoever migrates in the Way of Allaah, he will find many dwelling places and plenty (of sustenance) to live by. And whoever leaves his home as an emigrant unto Allaah and His Messenger, and death overtakes him, his reward is then surely incumbent upon Allaah, and Allaah is Ever Oft-Forgiving, Most Merciful." [Surah An-Nisaa: 100]

Hijrah is obligatory from the Land of Shirk to the Land of Islaam. This is especially the case if a person is not able to perform his worship in the most perfect of manners. The time period for Hijrah has not come to an end in spite of the Prophet's saying: **"There is no (more) Hijrah after the Conquest",** which means: "There is no more Hijrah from Makkah" since it had become a Land of Islaam.

But as for migrating from the Lands of Disbelief to the Lands of Islaam, then this remains in effect so long as the heavens and the earth remain in existence. This is why the Messenger of Allaah ﷺ said: **"Hijrah will not cease until repentance ceases. And repentance will not cease (to be accepted) until the sun rises from the place where it sets (i.e. the west)."**

So therefore the door of repentance remains open, and likewise, the door of Hijrah remains open until Allaah takes back the earth and those upon it. It is not permissible to delay in making Hijrah from a Land of Disbelief for the one who is able to do it. This is so that he won't be afflicted as regards to his Religion and prevented from the Path of Allaah. Rather, it is upon him to migrate to the Lands of Islaam and to expend his utmost effort to gain residency in (one of) the Lands of Islaam. [137]

---

[137] Refer to *Jaami' Shurooh al-Usool–uth-Thalaathah* (pg. 780-781)

Glossary of Terms Used in the Book

Adhaan	The Call to Prayer in Islaam.
Ahaadeeth	See Hadeeth
Ayaat	Lit. Sign - More commonly, this refers to verses from the Noble Qur'aan. Its singular form is *ayah*. It could also be used to refer to a sign or symbol.
Badr	Lit. Full moon - The terms "The Day of Al-Badr" or "The Battle of Badr" refers to the first battle that took place between the Muslims and the pagan Arabs of Makkah.
Bid'ah	Lit. Innovation - Commonly used to refer to something that is newly introduced into the Religion, which the Prophet and his Companions never did, even though they had the ability to do it.
Da'wah	Lit. Call - This refers to the concept and practical implementation of inviting and calling a person or persons to abide by and accept Islaam in its pure and unadulterated form.
Eemaan	Lit. Faith - To affirm the belief of everything that Allaah revealed through His Book, i.e. the Qur'aan, or upon the tongue of His Prophet, i.e. the Sunnah. More specifically, it is to believe in Allaah, His Angels, His revealed Books, His Messengers, the Day of Judgement, and the Divine Pre-Decree - the good and evil of it. Eemaan (Faith) is represented by a firm belief of the heart, action of the limbs, and a statement from the tongue. It increases by the performance of good deeds and decreases by the committal of sins.
Fataawaa	The plural form of *fatwa*. These are religious verdicts issued by scholars of Islaam, referred to as Muftees, which apply to the religious ruling on current events

	and matters. These rulings are derived from the Qur'aan, the Sunnah, the understanding of the Salaf, and scholarly Ijtihaad.
Fitnah	Pl. *Fitan*. This linguistically refers to calamities, trials, tribulations and mischief.
Hadeeth	Lit. Speech - A textual recorded narration containing information about one of the Prophet's sayings, actions or tacit approval of something. Such a report can either be authentic or weak, according to the grading and verification of the Muslim scholars.
Halaal	One of the five religious rulings according to the Principles of Fiqh. It refers to something that is lawful, i.e. the person who does it gets rewarded while the person who abandons it gets punished. It can also generally refer to something that Allaah has made lawful, be it a concept, practice, food, interaction, and so on.
Hamzah	One of the letters of the Arabic alphabet, which is characterized as a glottal stop. It can be used as an interrogatory marker, i.e. when it stands alone at the beginning of a sentence it turns that sentence into a question.
Haraam	One of the five religious rulings according to the Principles of Fiqh. It refers to something that is unlawful, i.e. the person who does it gets punished while the person who abandons it gets rewarded. It can also generally refer to something that Allaah has made unlawful and prohibited, be it a concept, practice, food, interaction, and so on.
Ijtihaad	When a scholar strives hard and expends his effort to derive a ruling for a matter that is not clearly apparent from the revealed texts.

Imaam	Lit. Leader - Most commonly used to refer to the person leading the congregational prayer. It also refers to the leader of a country or state, i.e. someone with authority. It is also used to refer to renowned Muslim scholars of the past and near present.
Irsaal	See Mursal
Islaam	Lit. Submission - The only true religion that Allaah has mandated upon mankind, and which He will accept on the Day of Judgement. The pure and correct form of Islaam is defined by the Qur'aan and the Sunnah, according to the practical understanding of the first three righteous generations of Muslims: The Sahaabah (Companions of the Prophet), the Taabi'een (Successors to the Companions), and the Atbaa' at-Taabi'een (Followers of the Successors).
Khaleefah	Lit. Successor - The title given to the supreme Muslim ruler under whom all of the Muslims gather under in obedience and loyalty.
Marfoo'	Lit. Raised - A report that has been "raised" up or ascribed to the Prophet. It is divided into two categories: *Marfoo' Sareeh,* which is a statement, action, tacit approval, or physical characteristic that has been ascribed to the Prophet; and *Marfoo' Hukm,* which is a report containing a ruling that is ascribed to the Prophet.
Masjid	Pl. Masaajid. The place where Muslims gather to worship and pray to Allaah. Known in English as Mosques, these are the Houses of Allaah.
Muhaajir	Lit. Emigrant - This can either refer to a person that abandons his country for another, regardless of what his intention is, or one who abandons something evil for the sake of Allaah.

Muhaddith	A scholar of Hadeeth.
Mujtahid	A scholar that has the ability and qualifications to perform Ijtihaad
Mursal	A narration that a Sahaabee (Companion) or a Taabi'ee (Successor) raised, i.e. ascribed, to the Prophet but yet did not hear it directly from him.
Mutawaatir	A narration reported by a large group of people, making it practicably impossible for them to have conspired to come up with a lie.
Quraysh	One of the several Arab tribes in Makkah. The Prophet Muhammad came from this particular tribe, which was dignified for its high status and rank.
Qur'aan	The Book that Allaah revealed to Muhammad for all of mankind and the jinn. It is the speech of Allaah and it is not created.
Rak'ah	A unit of prayer or the actual bowing position within prayer.
Saheeh	Lit. Correct/Authentic - A grading term for a narration that is authentically attributed to the Prophet.
Salaf	Lit. Predecessors - This refers to the first three generations of Islaam: The Sahaabah, the Taabi'een, and the Atbaa' at-Taabi'een. These were the first three virtuous generations of Islaam about whom the Prophet said: **"The best of people is my generation, then those that come after them, then those that come after them."**
Shahaadah	This refers to the testimony of faith, by which one enters into Islaam if uttered with firm belief. It is: "I bear witness that there is no deity that has the right to be worshipped except Allaah and that Muhammad is His slave and messenger." This represents the pure

monotheistic faith.

Sharee'ah	In general, this refers to the Religion of Islaam. Specifically, it refers to the laws and governing system of Islaam.
Surah	Pl. Suwar. A chapter from the Noble Qur'aan.
Sunnah	Lit. Way - The way and guidance of Prophet Muhammad, as represented in his speech, action, and tacit approval, which have been recorded and transmitted in reports and narrations known as Hadeeth.
Taaghoot	This refers to everything that is worshipped besides Allaah, while at the same time being pleased with this worship.
Tafseer	The interpretation of the meanings of the Qur'aan.
Ummah	Lit. Nation - The nation of Muslims as a whole, past or present and consisting of all those who ascribe truthfully to Islaam.